Faith Over Fear

Michael S. O`Neil
Faith Over Fear
Forged Through Fire

Published by BooXAI

ISBN: 978-965-578-782-5

Faith Over Fear

Forged Through Fire

Michael S. O`Neil

For Sadie

Contents

Acknowledgments

I cannot begin my acknowledgments without first acknowledging and thanking Jesus Christ, Our Lord and Savior. For without Him, this story would not be possible. I thank God for everything, great and small. I am most gracious to serve Him in His Name!

The following names are among my influencers and helped me along my path. I encourage those reading this book to look up the names of some of those I present thanks to. It was because of them, through God's influence, that I am where I am today spiritually. I list these names in no particular order.

Thomas & Diana Duebelbeis
The Bonallie Family
Shari McGriff
Annette Rowe
Boyd Zeigler
Robert Duebelbeis
Gunnar & Lila Nelson
Shari St. Louis
Tommy Duebelbeis

Henry & Lana Breaux
Cade & Marlena
Kathleen Duebelbeis
Min Yeo
Monique MacKay
Juan O. Savin
David Nino Rodriguez
Jodie Ledgerwood
Michael Jaco
Chris Eryx
Wendy Dominski
Jon Herold
Mike Lindell
Scott Russell
Scott McKay
LTG Mike Flynn
Brian Brase
Mike Adams
LTG McInerny
Mike Landus
Mel K
Kash Patel
PioyPioyPioy
Tom Numbers
Barb Petersen
Pastor Locke
LT (And We Know)
Relentless Truth
The Trumps

Dave at X-22
Scotty Mar10
Dr. Peter McCullogh
Sal72H
Adam Akroyd
Dr. Robert Malone
You Guys on Telegram
Dark Knight
Robert F. Kennedy, Jr.
Candace Fisher
Scotty's Cousin
Kristy Roan
Ann Dorn
Arv Danielson
Lori Shulte
Lauren Hawley
Shawn Nelson
Kelly Scriber
Michael Snider
Josh & Nicole McAfee
Tom Renz
Lynne Snider
Absolute Conviction
Dwayne Cooney
Doug Hawley
Feisty Cat
Steve Bannon
B Hawley
Coach Mel

Cara Mathes
Rob B.
Vickie Weir
Marilee Winter-Sauer
Karen B.
Sherry Ford
Dawn Geile-Gavin
Rebecca Newton
Joel Colombero
Joan Montague
Anna Gostevskyh
Scott Kestersen
Mercedes O'Neil

I know I am missing a ton of people to acknowledge here. Many people have diligently continued to get the word out to the masses about the truth that has been censored by those who wish to do us harm. This book would not be possible from the many thousands of hours of research because of Patriots like you, who diligently dig and present the truth to all of us. It is because of the collective efforts of everyone in this fight that the Old Guard will tumble. I look forward to that day!

Introduction

Have you ever awakened from a dream only to find out you are living in a nightmare? That is what I felt happened in the aftermath of COVID-19. I was living in Hawaii, working for the Department of the Army as a Department of the Army Civilian in an Army Four-Star Command. Geographically separated from my family for a decade, the COVID-19 narrative brought me to my knees. I was skeptical of the origins from the beginning. By the time I departed Hawaii and Federal Service due to the illegal and unconstitutional vaccine mandate, I lost everything it took my entire adult life to earn.

Over the last four years, and much longer, to be honest, we have been lied to. We have been lied to about COVID-19, the 2020 election, January 6th, and so much more. The result has been catastrophic for the entire world, yet many are living under some mass formation psychosis. These people have unfortunately been programmed all their lives by a media that lies to all of us. The media manipulation, especially against the 45th President of the United States, has been nothing short of sinister. Do you remember when Donald J. Trump was beloved by many within the media and entertainment industry? Politicians and influencers such as Whoopie Goldberg and Oprah Winfrey? Many of the hip hop artists rapped about him. Why, all of the sudden, would they all turn on him once he came down that escalator? Was there something he knew that these people of influence didn't want to come out?

This is my personal story of what I went through from the tyrannical lockdowns in Hawaii, the results of the Manchurian candidate installed in the White House, my leaving a job I loved and becoming homeless, and all of the things I endured until now. I am sure, regardless of where you find yourself across the political spectrum, most of you have been through quite a struggle over the past few years. What if that struggle was due to the manipulation of a few so that they could control the masses? What if all of those who claim to represent us, regardless of political party, do not support We the People at all?

This book is about how I saw things since the beginning of the COVID-19 lockdowns from my point of view. I present several different topics, more so than I stated above. I felt compelled to present to you, the reader, everything in my soul. Before I began this long and difficult journey, I knew God was real. It was only after losing everything that I realized how real He actually is, and I have listened to Him or tried to listen, every step of the way since. I have learned that I may not have a lot, but in walking with Him, I have everything! This book would not be possible without Him.

The beginning starts at the US/Canadian Border after driving north on Interstate 15. The timeframe was August 2022, almost three years after COVID-19 swept the world. I was utterly shocked at the treatment I received, yet I remained calm during my interrogation. Once this story is revealed, we will go back to where it all began in Hawaii. This story is just a snapshot. You may find yourself agreeing with some things while vehemently disagreeing with others, and that's okay. I aim to get you thinking, "what if?" I strongly suggest that if you feel something is not right, look deeper into the subjects I address and research the names of those I have acknowledged. The names that appear in this book are the names that have been censored all over the Media, Big Tech, Social Media, and by politicians from all sides who do not have our interests at heart. We are living in The Great Awakening, and the truth is messy, but it is also necessary. I want to thank you for your interest! WHERE WE GO ONE, WE GO ALL!

Chapter 1

Flash Forward

"Do not pray for an easy life. Pray for the strength to endure a difficult one."
-Bruce Lee

Late in the evening of August 23, 2022, about an hour before sunset, I reached the town of Shelby, Montana, located approximately 35 miles south of the Sweetgrass-Coutts border of Canada. My car's front grill and windshield were covered with bugs, so I decided to get a car wash after refueling. I remember pulling into the full-service car wash about five minutes before closing time. I only realized I was the last customer when I noticed the workers closing things up. I gave the attendant a tip, headed out to Interstate 15, and continued my trek north.

The journey on I-15 past Shelby towards the Canadian border is pretty desolate, and it was a boring ride since there isn't much in terms of life on this stretch. At this time of night on a Tuesday, there wasn't much traffic coming from either direction. I was driving within five miles of the speed limit, and there were not more than a handful of cars that passed me going north. While driving, I looked to the west and saw a wall of clouds in the distance and a very peculiar view of the sun peeking through the clouds as it slowly descended towards the horizon. As I drove and peeked in that direction, I couldn't help but notice an eerie resemblance to the Eye of Sauron from the Lord of the Rings Trilogy, staring back at me through the clouds. I will never forget the picture implanted in my head witnessing this, as it gave me a surreal and sobering feeling. A few minutes later I looked at my odometer by chance and noticed it read 116666 miles. I realize that everything is connected by numbers, and though totally out of my area of expertise, this type of stuff completely fascinates me. I immediately thought of my vaccination card that I placed in *Daniel Chapter One*. Was I about to enter the Lion's Den? The signs were screaming at me, yet I pressed on as God was with me in the passenger seat.

I reached the border shortly after 9:00 pm Tuesday and waited behind a line of traffic awaiting entry into Canada. I reached the gate approximately thirty minutes later and talked with the guard. He was a young man, most likely in his late twenties or early thirties, and was good-looking, with dark hair and a thin build. He asked me for my identification, so I gave him my retired status military identification card. Looking at the card, he asked me if I had a second form of identification, so I pulled out my Missouri driver's license and gave it to him.

"What brings you to Canada?" the guard asked.

"I am visiting my girlfriend in Edmonton," I replied.

"Where do you live and work? We ask these questions because there are people who come up to Canada and stay here illegally," he replied.

"I currently live in St. Peters, Missouri and work at a Christian T-shirt factory named Elly & Grace in High Ridge, Missouri," I stated.

We continued the small talk for a few minutes, and I figured I was about to be let through when he asked me about ArriveCAN. Remembering what Vickie, my Canadian-American dual-citizen friend, told me about ArriveCAN, I played the dumb American and acted like I wasn't aware of its existence.

He asked me to pull my vehicle into the parking lot around the corner, to answer a few questions from the immigration officer inside before I continued my journey. I parked in the stall around the corner in front of the door and went inside. At this point, I wasn't sure if the guard I talked to raised any red flags about me to his co-workers, but I remained calm, cool, and collected, walking inside with confidence. After all, I just wanted to cross the border and see my girlfriend.

While inside, the immigration officer asked me some questions about what my purpose was in visiting Canada. He repeated the questions the guard at the gate asked, along with how long I had planned to stay, who I was visiting, where I was going, etc. I noticed a bit of adversarial behavior from him as he asked me these questions. I showed no bother, as I figured the immigration officers asked everyone questions in such a manner before allowing them to go forward. He told me he needed to search my car, as standard procedure. Still, I was not worried, as I was used to this type of screening from traveling overseas.

As I sat and waited for the officer to return, I did some internet surfing and texted Anna back and forth. I hadn't sent her too many messages since she was in Calgary celebrating her daughter's birthday. We both agreed the best thing for me was to find a motel somewhere not far from the border crossing. I was to pick her up the next day around noon, as the drive was about three hours and twenty minutes from the border. I must have waited more than forty-five minutes before the immigration officer returned. As I sat in the waiting room, I told Anna I didn't think that was a good sign.

Finally, the immigration officer returned with his immediate supervisor. The supervisor was a woman probably in her early 30s with dark hair, slicked back and held in a tight bun, and her height was approximately 5'7. She stood close but was behind the officer and slightly to the side. He asked most of the questions, but she did chime in with questions of her own from time to time. For a third time, I was asked the same questions, only now the questions were a little more in-depth. I knew at this point it would be difficult to cross over into Canada, and I mentioned that to Anna while I was waiting for their return from searching my vehicle.

"What is the name of the person you wish to see?" he asked. I gave him her full name.

"What is the purpose of your visit?" he questioned.

"I just want to see my girlfriend in Edmonton," I replied. "I only plan to stay in Canada for a week."

He then asked, "Where did you meet her and how long have you known each other?"

I knew they must have found something in my car

because the questions began to sound more like an interrogation. At this point, I was thinking that the likelihood of my passing through immigration and continuing my journey north was fading fast. The last time I visited Canada, I did not receive the criminal treatment I did on this night, but I was wearing the full Armor of God and remained steadfast.

"I met her while livestreaming on Facebook for the convoy," I replied.

"The Freedom Convoy? You were in the Freedom Convoy?" the supervisor piped in.

Not thinking anything of it, since there were multiple convoys in America before the merge in Hagerstown, I inadvertently made a mistake by telling them I was with the Freedom Convoy. I did not realize then that the trucker protest held in Ottawa earlier in the year was labeled "The Freedom Convoy." When they heard me say I was a part of the Freedom Convoy, all the bells and whistles went off in their heads. I later learned a large group of truckers shut down Highway 4 around the village of Coutts. From here, the interrogation became much more adversarial, yet I still maintained my cool. It felt so good to have God next to me as this went on because without Him, I most likely would have cracked under pressure.

"We looked through your car and found quite a bit of anti-vax paraphernalia. Why would someone who received the Covid vaccination be anti-vax?" asked the officer.

I didn't think in a million years that my car would be rifled through when crossing the border; otherwise, I would have left my belongings in St. Louis and traveled with only a travel bag. I had no idea that America's sister country to the north had become a communist state, but here I was, witnessing a communist interrogation first-hand. I replied to his question in the most professional way that I possibly could. "There are many people that have received the shot and received many different types of injuries as a result of the shot. People regret getting it," I said. "I regret getting it," knowing this was a complete fabrication on my part.

I was amazed at the blank stares I received after telling them this information. It was almost as if their expressions were robotic like they didn't compute what I had just delivered to them. I didn't even go down the road of telling them that the shot was responsible for many thousands of deaths that would be attributed to "dying suddenly." It was about this time the supervising officer pulled out my Take Action USA business card and asked me to explain exactly what kind of organization Take Action USA was. I'm sure they knew about Take Action Canada because they placed anti-vax stickers all across the country and made their presence known in many other ways as well.

I explained that Take Action USA was a grassroots organization designed to bring groups together to peacefully and professionally protest at rallies in America over the vaccine mandates that were not in accordance with the US Constitution and American values. I also explained that our organization was the type to also bring different churches together and provide a network that preached in the spirit of the Bible as written. I explained that as Inspector General, I was interested in the transparency and accountability of TAUSA, and our IGs are placed at every level to ensure transparency within the organization.

"Do you plan on protesting while you are in Canada?" she asked.

"No," I answered. "I only want to visit with my girlfriend."

"Ok," said the immigration officer. "We found some things which we thought were questionable, but I see no reason to decline you from entering Canada."

"Thank you very much," I responded, as I gathered my notebook full of information from TAUSA meetings they brought in from the car. "Thank you for your service."

"Oh, one more thing," said the officer. "I'm going to need you to show me your vaccination status."

"No problem, officer," I replied, as I pulled up the picture on my phone to show him.

He took the phone and studied it carefully, asking, "Do you have a hard copy of this?"

"Yes, I do, sir. It's out in the car. I'll have to go get it," I said.

So I took my phone from him and went out to the

car to retrieve the vaccination card. I couldn't believe it was this difficult to get into Canada over a simple shot. How much more authoritarian can things be that a person cannot go anywhere without providing documentation of a medical procedure? Things couldn't be any more intrusive and tyrannical. I walked out to my car, opened the trunk, opened my backpack, retrieved the family Bible, and returned inside. While inside, I plopped the Bible on the counter in front of the two officers and opened it to the Book of Daniel, where the card was placed at random a few days prior before I departed St. Louis.

"Here you go," I said, and gave the card to him. He looked at it for about two seconds before his supervisor took the card from him and examined it for its thickness. I knew exactly what she was doing. When I first handled a COVID-19 vaccine card, I noticed its thickness was like that of a playing card. This was definitely not of the same stock, but it was close, so that was why I used it.

"This is not the appropriate stock," she said.

I replied, "Well, that's the one I received, so I really don't know what to say."

Her subordinate chimed in, "Do you have an immunization record that you can show me?"

I thought this question was a step too far. After all, one's immunization record can go back quite a few years. I didn't have my immunization readily handy.

Even if I did, this was quite intrusive. So I said, "I don't really feel comfortable with giving you that information." I must have made her angry with this answer because she became very stern with me.

"This man is an Immigration Officer in the country of Canada!" she exclaimed. "If you wish to come into this country, he has every right to ask you this question if you want to pass through!"

"Okay," I replied. "But I don't have that documentation on my person."

She looked at the vaccine card and asked, "Where did you receive your vaccination?"

"Trippler Army Medical Center Honolulu, Hawaii, ma'am," I replied.

"I am going to call them and find out if this card is real or not," she stated.

"That's fine," I replied coolly, knowing she called my bluff but staying completely calm.

I walked fifteen feet and sat in the chair. By this time, it was after 11:00 pm local time, five hours ahead of Hawaii. I sat in the chair with the Armor of God and texted Anna, telling her that the authorities called my bluff and were calling Hawaii to verify my vaccination status for COVID-19. I was a bit upset inside, not because she called my bluff, but because I was unable to visit my girlfriend, whom I soon after found out was suffering from Stage 4 cancer. She was dying, but I wasn't aware of that at this point, and I think Anna might have been in denial about her status. Could I have mentioned my girlfriend was suffering from cancer? I think had I mentioned it, there wouldn't have been a difference. These folks did their job well, unfortunately for me. However, I was about to find out that God had different plans for me. Had I not left St. Louis almost two days prior, I would not be on the journey I later found myself. Unfortunately, Anna could only share with me from afar, and what happened at the border was hard on us both, but I think more so for her.

The Immigration Officer and his supervisor returned and called me to the counter about thirty minutes later. He told me he called Trippler Army Medical Center, but it was after hours, and the records clerk was not at work. The person he talked to stated that it was not possible to go into the database with the clerk gone and stated they had upgraded the system in September of 2021. The information on my card stated I received the vaccine in August of that year. God was looking out for me because who knows what would have happened had they proven I had shown a fake vaccination card. Some people I told the story to afterward thought it was possible I could have done jail time for that. Anyway, the officer told me that since they couldn't find proof of my vaccination, they couldn't let me cross. He told me that if I came back the next morning after 8:00 am with proof I was vaccinated, they would let me through. He gave me a slip showing my refusal status in the country and sent me on my way.

This is the story of how I survived the COVID-19

lockdown in Hawaii and everything that happened after that. COVID-19 resulted in the downfall of a 27-year marriage, a stolen election, the loss of a career due to mandatory vaccination, and other heartbreaks. My story is of faith in God and the will to trust and give everything to Him, even when all seems lost.

I'm sure many people will be able to relate to my story and become inspired to keep walking in faith. To keep going when you feel you can go no further. He is all around us, and He talks to us. We just have to listen. Let me go back to the beginning, only a few months before the infamous Covid lockdown that almost tore us all apart.

I arrived in Hawaii from Korea in November 2019. I was excited about my new assignment on the IG Staff that served the United States Army Pacific Command (USARPAC) Commanding General. This is a Four-Star billet in command of all US Army units within the Pacific Rim. Some places include units stationed in Korea, Japan, Guam, Hawaii, Alaska, and Washington State. The USARPAC IG consisted of two main departments; the Assistance & Investigations Department, which I worked in, and the Inspections Department. Our staff consisted of 12 people, and our lead IG, the Command IG (CIG), was an advisor to the Four-Star Commander. Our office provided oversight to the IG offices at the lower echelons in USARPAC, and we communicated regularly to the Department of the Army Inspector General Office.

I was excited about my new position. Working at this level was sure to give me the exposure I sought to move up in the civilian ranks. By this time, I had built a very positive reputation through my work. The IG folks in Hawaii knew who they were hiring, as they could view my case notes for their thoroughness and witness my impartiality on the cases in which I worked. I was not perfect, but I constantly strived for that perfection. There was no question as to whether or not I gave my all when it came to providing assistance not only to those seeking it but to those leaders who pushed that envelope.

I remember spending Thanksgiving on the Island of Oahu by myself. I was a bit surprised at being the new guy that no one from the office had invited me over to their house for Thanksgiving. I wasn't offended in the least, but I did feel a little awkward since it is usually customary to invite single soldiers over to these types of dinners when they are not with family. I took the opportunity to go hiking since I have always been interested in that hobby. After the hike, my Thanksgiving dinner was a double quarter pounder with cheese meal at McDonald's.

My life was pretty routine and consisted of gym in the early morning and arrival at work around 8:00 am at the office, about an hour before most of the military would show up. The staff consisted of eight military members and four civilians. All of us were military retirees. Each day, we would enter the IG database to look at active cases of the lower-echelon Command IGs and provide guidance when warranted. This job was not difficult, and sometimes I would look for other work since there wasn't much to do on a day-to-day basis. I was used to going to units and providing information for the leadership and the soldiers, but that wasn't the mission here. We would give weekly updates to the CIG on issues involving allegations of senior ranking officials anywhere within the command. The CIG would then brief the Commanding General.

It was the end of 2019, and my wife and I had lived separately for more than seven years. I was able to attend my daughter's high school graduation, but I, unfortunately, missed her graduation from college. I was in Afghanistan during all of that time. I am proud of my daughter, Mercedes. She currently lives and works in Oklahoma City as a probation and Parole Officer, and she is very good at what she does.

I had told my wife repeatedly that I missed her and did not want to continue the separation away from her, which is why I left Afghanistan in 2017. We were at the end of 2019, still apart from each other. I had not been a perfect husband, and she knew that, but I told her I couldn't live like this any longer. Anyway, at this time, we were still talking over Facetime weekly. We chose to speak at the same time weekly because we both agreed long ago in Afghanistan that if we talked more often, we would wind up with nothing to discuss. So we limited it to weekends unless there was something important.

Since Hawaii was not considered an overseas assignment for DA Civilians (it is for the military), the government would not provide free housing like I received in Korea. Because of this, I was unsure how far my money would stretch. Keep in mind my service level was GS-12, and I needed to support two households. At least my house in Oklahoma was paid off, thanks to my time in Afghanistan, but my wife still had to live and had three pets to take care of. So, I found an apartment with no air conditioning, which charged $1900 monthly rent. I was willing to do this, knowing that I would still be able to make enough to pay all the bills. I was also aiming to spend my time in Hawaii before returning to Korea.

In early January 2020, I noticed a pain in my lower abdomen while working out at the gym. After I conducted some research, I made an appointment to visit the doctor. I think I gave myself a hernia while working out. I immediately ceased going to the gym, as I didn't want to aggravate things more than necessary. Things seemed to worsen over the waiting period before my appointment with certain movements. I was seen a few days later, and the doctor verified my inguinal hernia, but he gave me a bonus and said I had a double inguinal hernia. Yes, both sides needed a surgical procedure. He gave me two options; make an appointment for surgery at Trippler Army Medical Center and wait until May, or get a consultation to see a local doctor. I chose the latter and waited for notification from the local clinic to come in for a consultation.

My consultation was scheduled for the second week of February. I noted that she was very professional and just a likable person overall. She looked at the area and then briefed me on what to expect. In the end, she gave me an appointment date for the hospital visit for surgery. The date was February 28, and though it seemed like a long time to deal with the pain, I knew I could deal with it because I had no other choice.

The day came for me to go into surgery, and one of my office mates picked me up from my apartment and took me to the hospital. The last thing I remember was having the mask put on my face and being told to count down from a hundred. I think I only made it to ninety-six before I was out. It must have gone smoothly because I didn't feel too bad afterward. They had me on some good pain medication, so there was zero chance of driving home myself. I called the office, was picked up again, and was escorted home. I was given two weeks of Convalescent Leave to recover.

My recovery was speedy. I was given a three-day supply of Oxycodone and, I think ten days of an antibiotic. My doctor said I would be sore for a couple of days, but truthfully, I don't remember feeling much soreness outside of the first day. I remember after the first day or two I did a video chat with my wonderful friends from Korea, Nav and Luanna, both Canadian expatriates who lived in Seoul. They worked as teachers to foreign students whose parents worked in the Canadian

Embassy. We had a beautiful relationship, and I consider those two my lifelong friends.

The XFL (Extreme Football League) started its inaugural season in February 2020, and Saint Louis was one of the eight cities that hosted a team. This invigorated all of us in Saint Louis since many of us were very sour about the Rams owner, Stan Kroenke, and how things played out over the years until he moved the team back to Los Angeles. This new league was fascinating, and it had some pretty exciting rules. The name of our new team was the St. Louis Battlehawks. Out of the eight cities, St. Louis had the most fans in the stadium every week. They played four weeks before the start of the COVID-19 virus, which caused everything in the world to lock down.

I was told by my doctor that I could do some light activity over the next two weeks, so I had enough room in my apartment to walk around continuously. It had three bedrooms. I had picked up a second bed in Korea, so I had two rooms with beds, and the third I used for an exercise room with an elliptical. I would walk around the living room and then go into the hallway, in and out of the spare rooms, and back to the living room. Sometimes, I did this continuously while the news or music was on, and sometimes, when I watched the XFL, I waited for the commercials, and then I would do my rounds. There were quite a few days during this period where I would log over 30,000 steps. I could tell it worked because I kept my weight close to what it had been before my injury.

I was paying close attention to the coronavirus news at the beginning of March. The pandemic was not declared, but the media would give new case numbers daily. The death count was beginning to rise as well. At this point, I was not fearful of catching anything. The narrative had already been told that those within the high-risk areas were those with compromised immune systems. I was still relatively young, not yet fifty, and in good health with zero comorbidities. I felt a little uneasy because something about this didn't feel right, yet I couldn't put my finger on why I felt the way I did. I remember a friend mentioning Event 201 on Facebook, and he said to look it up. I blew it off at this point, though I wish I hadn't, for it was a foretelling of things to come.

On March 11, 2020, the World Health Organization (WHO) declared COVID-19 a pandemic. Two days later, President Trump declared a national emergency and placed a travel ban on non-US citizens traveling from Europe. That Monday, March 16th, I returned to work. Leadership talked about the looming lockdown, and we completed the necessary training that week for us to be able to work from home. So, here I am, coming back to work, only to go back home again for who knows how long (It amounted to about fifteen months). The CIG stated we would have ⅓ of the office at work at any given time because we still needed personnel for people who needed assistance. In the Assistance and Investigations Branch, that meant one day a week in the office for all of us since there were five on the team. I found out quickly that working from home in an office that mostly provides oversight was not a healthy idea, since there was not much work to do at our level. I will talk more about that in the next chapter.

KAMEHAMEHA I

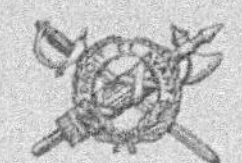

Department of the Army

I, Michael S. O'Neil,

having been assigned as an Inspector General, do solemnly swear (or affirm) that I accept the special obligations and responsibilities of the position freely, that I will uphold the standards for Inspectors General prescribed by regulations and that I will, without prejudice or partiality, discharge the duties of the office upon which I am about to enter. So help me God.

Inspector General

Date:

Sworn in Recognition of Special Trust and Honor by Order of THE SECRETARY OF THE ARMY

The Inspector General

Secretary of the Army

Chapter 2

The Pandemic

On March 23rd, Hawaii Governor David Ige issued a stay-at-home order due to the rising cases of COVID-19 in Hawaii. This would go into effect at midnight on the 24th. Though we were on lockdown, things still seemed normal in the beginning. I had no idea what things were going to turn into, and never in a million years thought this was going to last as long as it did. Each day, we had to check in with our leadership to make sure everything was okay. That check-in was usually in the form of a text. The command allowed us leeway in leaving during the day to get essentials like groceries or medicine but working from home was the new normal.

I remember going to the commissary in Honolulu, near the Navy Exchange, looking for toilet paper. Toilet paper on the island was scarce, which I ran low on during my recovery. I felt as if people who hoarded toilet paper at the time were very inconsiderate of others and couldn't for the life of me figure out why people were buying it all up. I traveled to many places on the island, Walmart, Sam's, Costco, and other military commissaries, and could not find any. Luckily, after telling the story to the maintenance man at my apartment complex, he gave me a couple of rolls.

Because of my injury, I was not in the shape I had been in when I arrived a couple of months prior. I hadn't gained any weight, but I could feel my body yearning to go to the gym. The week before the lockdown order by the governor, I began going back to the gym and took things very easy. The result of the lockdown, coupled with the second lockdown in late August, would be highly detrimental to my health. The order kept all parks, beaches, gyms, and high-traffic areas closed. I could not work out at the gym or go hiking, which bothered me since I found out there were not a lot of people around when I hiked in many of the areas on the island, with the exception of the tourist attractions, such as the Diamond Head on the east side of Oahu. Those who went to the beach were cited by the Honolulu Police Department. It didn't take long before I realized living on the island was the worst place I could be living in isolation during the pandemic.

On March 30th, the Food and Drug Administration (FDA) authorized the use of Hydroxychloroquine for Emergency Use Authorization (EUA). This was an interesting development, as this drug had been used for many decades against malaria. The Department of Defense (DOD) issued this drug for all personnel deployed to the Middle East and Africa. Prior to my deployment to Afghanistan in 2012, I was issued what amounted to a year's worth of Hydroxychloroquine. I had not heard about this authorization at the time. I only heard about it when a Jewish doctor from New York produced a video of himself making a plea to President Trump, stating he had already treated hundreds of patients with a cocktail of Hydroxychloroquine, Vitamin D3, Azithromycin (an antibiotic), and Zinc. The name of this doctor was Dr. Vladimir Zelenko.

With the revelation of the success of using this drug and President Trump touting the success Doctor Zelenko had achieved came an onslaught of propaganda against the use by the media. Keep in mind that the FDA approved the use of this drug, but the media came up with distortions about how Hydroxychloroquine was dangerous and caused heart problems. I knew immediately that this story was false. Hydroxychloroquine had been safely used for decades to fight against Malaria. Why would the DOD issue this drug to millions of personnel over the years if it causes heart problems? I took this drug while deployed as a contractor in Afghanistan and never had an issue, nor did I hear anyone else having an issue. But suddenly, when President Trump touts this drug, it's dangerous.

I remember having debates with a couple of liberal friends from Korea. Travis and Finn were both expats

I'd known for years. Each would tell me how dangerous this drug was. Travis went even further and would send me studies on the drug. I was on top of this, though, and I would scour the internet for new news. When a study was released, I would read it and then debunk him. One study from Brazil touted how, in clinical trials, the cocktail killed a number of people. I read the amount that was given to the patients, and it was way too much. Dr. Zelenko recorded the right dosage levels to administer to patients, but the levels I noticed in this study were extreme. To me, this seemed like an orchestrated effort to sabotage Dr. Zelenko's findings. The Zelenko Protocol Table is provided with other photos at the end of the chapter.

Similarly, Travis pointed out to me the Lancet study on the dangers of Hydroxychloroquine. Again, I had already read the study prior to him passing it along. Nowhere in the study did I find any dosage rates for Hydroxychloroquine, Vitamin D3, Zinc, or Azithromycin. I told Travis that I thought this study was incomplete because of the lack of dosage data. In both instances, he could not refute what I gave him. However, like many others, he would not wake up against the media narrative. Not long afterward, Lancet retracted the study because the data could not be vouched for. I'm no doctor and have never studied in the field, but I find it very difficult to believe a person of my stature could get it right, yet medical researchers could not.

"What is really going on with this?" I thought. I think the whole Hydroxychloroquine and Ivermectin issue made me pause about whether or not we were being lied to regarding the COVID-19 narrative. Unfortunately, this narrative is what alienated me and many others among family and friends. Some of us could see through the lies and propaganda, while many could not.

The first couple of months of the lockdown were not too bad in terms of restlessness. There wasn't much going on, and I continued to go to work once a week. We didn't have a lot of work since everything pretty much stopped all over the world. There were not a lot of IG assistance cases in the IG database, and we rarely had any phone calls or physical visits from soldiers in Hawaii. I found myself in the deputy's office regularly, just talking about what was going on in the world with Covid and how Trump was handling things. Dan was a Trump fan as well, so we talked a lot about how the media continuously made attempts to thwart his decision making at every turn. Of the twelve members in our office, I would have to say Trump had about fifty percent support. This surprised me, as I remember coming up through the ranks; the Army was much more conservative in the 1990s than it was after I retired in 2010. I saw that in 2017 when I was at Fort Bliss, Texas, and I noticed the complaints soldiers came to us with were much different than they were just seven years before. Still, I was happy to be in this job, as I could help young soldiers and leaders.

As time went on, the lack of work and the lack of human interaction began to take a toll on my physical, mental, and spiritual well-being. As I've stated, I had no family or friends to hang out with. My friend and former Platoon Leader, Major (MAJ) Minh Nguyen, was stationed there, and though we hung out together when I first arrived, we rarely saw each other for another year. I became somewhat of a whiskey connoisseur while stationed at Fort Bliss in 2017 and continued dabbling with different types of whiskey in Korea and Hawaii. I remember going to the local grocery store down the street from my apartment complex and buying a bottle in the evenings.

After a while, with nothing but time on my hands, I would drink nightly. It didn't take long before my habit would result in drinking half the bottle almost every night. If I wasn't in the store buying a new bottle every two days, I would be there every third day. Sometimes, I would buy a pint of ice cream and chocolate to go with it. What a combination that was! Knowing that I wouldn't have to be at work the next morning, I would stay up late watching the news or watching a movie because all I had to do to ensure that I was alive was to answer a morning text from my supervisor. Telephone conversations were a rarity at this point. I was really lucky that my abuse of alcohol didn't come back to haunt me in any way. I stayed at the apartment, so there was no worry of possible incidents behind the wheel of my car. I've never been violent, and there was no exception to this rule when it came to my drinking since I was always considered to be a 'happy' drunk. But what made things worse for me was the fact I was lonely.

I have had bouts of depression and anxiety my whole life, but nothing could be compared to the depression and anxiety I faced while living in this apartment alone. I experienced many peaks and valleys then; honestly, it still goes on more than three years later. My faith in God is what helped me survive. But I have to say, it hasn't been easy, and these three plus years have been the most challenging years of my life. Thank God my faith has been as strong as it has, otherwise, I don't think I would be writing this right now.

The first couple of months during the pandemic were relatively quiet. I don't remember much going on in the news. Every day the news was about the number of cases and the number of deaths. I was glued to my television every day while I was at home, watching Fox News broadcast Trump's daily briefs. Truth be told, it became tiring after a while listening to the same thing day in and day out. I don't fault him for this, as he was doing his job by briefing the American people. And we watched the programming daily, most of us anyway. I knew I needed to do something extra with my time, so I looked into pursuing a Doctorate Degree. American Military University/ American Public University (AMU/APU) was offering a degree in Global Security. I hadn't done any schooling since I completed my Master's Degree in 2010, so I thought it was time to get back into it to stay busy. I thought by doing this, I would keep my mind off of the growing number of deaths and tailor my drinking habit a little bit.

Part of the requirements for entering the program called for letters of recommendation and an essay completed and turned in as a Doctoral candidate. I requested what the essay needed to be about but received somewhat of a vague answer, which I can't recall. I decided to write about COVID-19 and used the information about the possibility of the use of a pandemic to release a bio-weapon worldwide to the public. In my estimation, writing about this was key to planning against terrorist organizations and state-sponsored terrorism, which is important in the world of Global Security. I also began learning German again because it was a requirement to graduate with a foreign language. In fact, the university required that the final presentation be done orally in a foreign language before awarding the degree. I felt slightly intimidated by this, but I was motivated to do so, and I signed up with Babel immediately to begin my German lessons.

The final step of the admissions process was an interview with members of AMU/APU. The interview was telephonic, and there were three members on the interview panel. The first interviewer was from the Office of Admissions. She asked me a few questions over a period of about ten minutes. Next was one of the professors at the college. He was a Special Forces officer in the rank of Lieutenant Colonel. He and I clicked immediately since we both served. He knew my IG background from when I told the three what I did for a living. Our conversation was smooth and steady. I thought since he was on the panel, given my credentials, I was a shoe in for the program. The final interviewer was the Global Security Program Director.

Prior to my interview, I reviewed the backgrounds of a few of the personnel I thought I might interview with. She was one of the people I looked at. When conducting my research, I noticed that she was a socialist, though she didn't blatantly come out and say this. However, being an investigator, I knew how to connect the dots. I bring this up because she asked me two questions: how do I get along with others? And how well do I conduct research? I remember telling her how I get along and telling her that I am driven when it comes to research. A few weeks later, I was rejected from the program. Part of me thinks the mentioning of possible bio-weapons from Senator Cotton (R-AR) and another quote from President Trump could have been the nail in my coffin. In any case, I look back on this and think the Lord intervened in this decision since my future path was to become very rocky and unknown. Imagine not completing my education program and owing thousands of dollars without having a way to pay for it.

For the first couple of months, it seemed like nothing happened. And then came George Floyd. With the whole world locked down and forced to stay home, there was no way to eliminate built-up tension or aggression.

Parks were closed, so there was no way to conduct any physical activity - no basketball, football, or soccer. I know the hell I went through, so I can imagine so many others getting into heavy drinking during the day and doing drugs. Almost everything was closed; however, the liquor stores remained open. The circumstances surrounding the pandemic and the lockdown that followed provided the means necessary for a proverbial Yellowstone eruption that followed after the killing of George Floyd.

On the 25th of May 2020 in Minneapolis, MN, a video emerged of Police Officer Derek Chauvin with his knee on the neck of George Floyd after a report of Floyd using a counterfeit twenty-dollar bill at a local store. The incident resulted in Floyd's death after numerous times of Floyd exclaiming, "I CAN'T BREATHE!" The incident sparked outrage all across America and the world. We had been on lockdown for more than two months now, and I believe this incident was the catalyst that started the summer of protests and heavy rioting across our great country. It was as if the COVID-19 lockdowns had produced a pot of boiling water, which erupted out of the pot and all over the stove.

Within days, protests rose everywhere, and things turned violent in many places. I was glued to my television during this period and was saddened, heartbroken, and frankly pissed off at the same time. By now, we had lived in this pandemic long enough and witnessed enough that I felt it was more of a "plandemic" than anything. And the mainstream news media didn't disappoint. Not long after the killing, cities across America were burning. Shameless CNN "journalists" were live on TV reporting about the "mostly peaceful" protests while cities were shown burning in the background. With the fanning of the flames by the media, law enforcement officials were being targeted just because they wore the uniform.

My home city of St. Louis did not escape the rioting. On the night of June 2, 2020, in the early hours of the morning, retired Police Captain David Dorn was killed by thugs as he stood guard outside of a friend's pawn shop. Not long after the incident, a video emerged of Captain Dorn lying in a pool of blood on the sidewalk, dying in real time. It was devastating to see the carnage happening in the city I grew up in. St. Louis, however, has been a city in decline for quite a few years.

I remember watching this on Fox News (the other media outlets didn't seem to want to give this story air time), as they covered this story extensively. Imagine wanting to protect a friend's livelihood after decades of serving and protecting the public, only to be snuffed out by the very people you swore an oath to protect. It is always so heartbreaking to see those in uniform being targeted by criminals, and I blame the mainstream media for fanning the flames with a certain narrative. I was introduced to his widow, Ann, by a mutual friend I worked for after I left Hawaii in late 2021 because of the illegal vaccine mandate for federal employees.

The summer of 2020 was marked by death and destruction all over America. It was absolute chaos. Those who weren't actively involved in the protesting and rioting were stuck in front of the television screen, watching many events unfold. I'm not going to rehash all of the violence in the summertime, but I remember seeing members of Antifa and Black Lives Matter tear up and destroy our country. And never forget that politicians urged people to donate money to release members arrested for their crimes, yet, January 6th protesters, who protested the results of the 2020 stolen election, are held against their will still today, violating their Sixth Amendment rights to a speedy trial. I remember hearing about damage estimates being in the billions after the riots stopped in the late summer of 2020.

Though chaos occurred throughout much of America, Hawaii was pretty docile. By June 19th, the governor allowed all gyms in Hawaii to re-open, with certain guidelines in place to avoid the risk of coronavirus spread. Unfortunately, I could not restart my earlier workout routines at the military base gyms. Active duty forces were given priority for the first couple of hours in the morning when it opened and again in the afternoon and early evening. All others were given the chance to work out during the off times when the military was at work. Since military personnel were also given priority on the weekends, I was forced to find a place to go in Honolulu. No disrespect to our military, but I was pretty upset the leadership chose to make things difficult for military retirees so they couldn't use the facilities. So, I bought a membership at Planet Fitness. They opened a bit later in the morning than the military gyms, but we worked from home. So I would show up when it opened at 5:00 am and worked out until about 7:15-7:30 am and then went home to shower and sit with my laptop on a dinner tray table in front of the television in my living room.

At first, things were fine at the gym. The rule was you had to wear a mask upon entering and have it on while going from machine to machine, but while working out at your machine, it could be removed. This worked for about the first two weeks before Planet Fitness changed the rules, making it so you had to wear your mask at all times. Even though my drinking had increased since the lockdown began, surprisingly, I was still in pretty decent shape. Even though I had to rebuild my muscles, my cardio was okay because I walked outside my apartment once I was sick of getting my steps inside. I remember not having much issue being on the treadmill while wearing a mask. I hated it because wearing the mask made me feel like an obedient slave, but it didn't give me problems at this time other than getting really wet to the point I had to go into the bathroom to dry it out after my cardio was complete.

This worked out quite well for a while. I remember at some point, I started going back in the afternoons sometimes because staying at home with little to do throughout the day was extremely boring. Sometimes, my boss would call me while I was on the treadmill. We would talk for a couple of minutes, and he knew I was working out, but he was cool with it all. I normally didn't leave the apartment before 3:00 pm to get my afternoon workout since I didn't want to appear like I wasn't doing anything during the day (which, normally, I wasn't doing much of anything anyway). This way, I would finish my workouts by 5:00 pm and be on the road home. I had to deal with rush hour traffic, but it was only a twenty-minute drive to reach my apartment.

On the 27th of August, Governor Ige instituted a second lockdown. This lockdown was a soul crusher. Again, I was isolated alone in my apartment with no human interaction. My motivation went down once more, and I was devastated that I could not get my workouts in. To me, these workouts were an incredible release for my soul. We were dealing with a propaganda narrative that this was a widespread killer, though the millions of flu cases each year just magically disappeared in 2020. I had one thing to help keep me from going insane and it was taken away in a flash. I could not believe how upside down the world had become, which would continue in the election season.

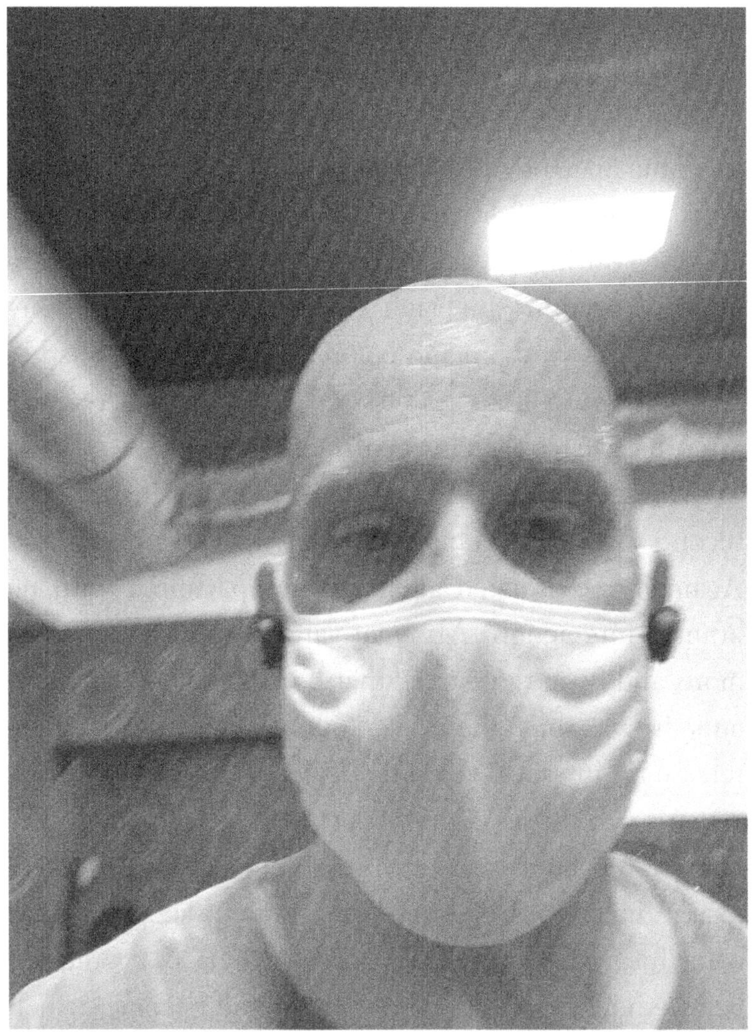

ZELENKO COVID19 PROTOCOL (moderate/high risk, > 45 yrs old)			
Items in orange are available OTC, others are prescription			
Prophylaxis			Treatment
1000mg, daily	Vitamin C	same	1000mg, 7 days
5000IU 125mcg, daily	Vitamin D3	double	10000IU 250mcg, 7 days OR 50000IU, 1-2 days
25mg, daily	Elemental Zinc	double	50mg, 7 days
	Zinc Ionophore		
500mg, daily	Quercetin	double	500mg, 2x - 7 days
OR		-	OR
400mg, daily	Epigallocatechin-gallate (EGCG)	same	400mg, 1x - 7 days
OR		-	OR
200mg, 5 days, 200-400mg weekly	Hydroxychloroquine (HCQ)	double	200mg, 2x - 5-7 days
OR		-	AND/OR
0.2mg/kg, day 1 & 3, weekly	Ivermectin (IVM)*	double	0.4-0.5mg/kg, 5-7 days
*Example: IVM dosage for 200lb person (90kg) - Prophylaxis 18mg, Treatment 36mg-45mg			
	Antibiotic		
---	Azithromycin (Z-PAK)	add	500mg, 1x - 5 days
			OR
---	Doxycycline	add	100mg, 2x - 7 days
	Other Treatment Options		
corticosteroid	Dexamethasone 6-12mg 1 time a day for 7 days or		
corticosteroid	Prednisone 20mg twice a day for 7 days, taper as needed		
corticosteroid	Budesonide 1mg/2cc solution via nebulizer twice a day for 7 days		
blood thinners	Blood thinners (i.e. Lovenox, Eliquis, Xarelto, Pradaxa, Aspirin)		
anti-inflammatory	Colchicine 0.6mg 2-3 times a day for 5-7 days		
	Monoclonal antibodies		
	Home IV fluids and oxygen		

SANDY MUCHOW

Mike–

Really glad that you joined our team! You've already made a big impact, and I'm sure you'll continue. Good luck w/ your doctoral program! Sandy

Chapter 3

Election Season

After the summer mayhem had ended in August, things began to quiet down. Both Trump and Biden began campaigning again earlier that summer, and now the campaigns were running at full speed. Frankly, I thought Trump did an outstanding job as president. Growing up, President Reagan was my favorite, but after seeing the accomplishments Trump completed in such a short time, I felt 45's performance during his term was beyond the pale. None of our adversaries around the world dared mess with us. If any enemy got out of line and threatened our interests overseas, that action was met with fire and fury. Iranian Quds Force Commander Qasem Soleimani was a recipient of this fury when he was killed by an airstrike in Baghdad at the beginning of the year. Though this happened, occasions such as these were rare.

In fact, with minor exceptions like Soleimani, this

was the first time in decades America had a president who, by and large, waged peace instead of using the might of the military to destabilize a region. The economy had roared until Covid and quickly rebounded when America re-opened, and so much more. I was proud as an American under Trump. Everything the media threw at him bounced off of him. Those who were indoctrinated by the mainstream media couldn't stand him, but for years, I could see through their lies and propaganda.

Once the political engine revved back up, Trump's rallies were huge. There were quite a few venues where his crowd sizes were immense. He would comment on how the media would refuse to turn their cameras to show the size of the crowds. The conservative news sites would show the size and always looked massive. The mainstream would always try to downplay the size of his crowds to make it look like Trump didn't have that much support, but in many of the videos I watched, his supporters showed up from all walks of life to his rallies. All I saw at Biden's rallies (if you want to call them rallies - more like family barbecues) were big circles with chairs and, in many cases, not more than fifty people attending. In my opinion, the whole Biden campaign was a sham. He truly campaigned from the basement.

Trump warned the American people on numerous occasions that the Democrats were going to cheat using the mail-in ballots. He made a bold claim that they would use COVID-19 as an excuse to usher in millions of mail-in ballots. It didn't take me long in 2020, after the lockdown, to figure out that COVID-19 was a scam perpetrated on the people of the world by the few billionaire families who control everything. This was about the time I learned and watched a film on Event 201, held at Johns Hopkins University in the fall of 2019, about two months prior to what we now know was a lab leak.

The event, sponsored by the Bill & Melinda Gates Foundation, ran a scenario of a virus creating a worldwide pandemic. Everything in this scenario played out, including what to do about disinformation. They were wargaming about what to do to combat possible narratives showing that this was a sham. And then this was released. Sounds sinister, doesn't it? Well, from what I've learned about this period and the period after, things were not how they seemed. I've heard accounts of people being infected with the biologically modified virus and sent on planes from China to major cities to spread coronavirus. Could this possibly be true? It would be an act of war if it were.

As the campaign went on, it was clear that this next election would be a lock for Donald J. Trump. Biden was just a weak candidate, and Trump's policies, strength, and moxy were just what America needed to continue forging ahead. I couldn't believe how strong this guy was. I mean, he spent four years putting up with lie after lie; if it wasn't the Russia hoax, it was the "very fine people" distortion of Charlottesville, or the upside-down Bible in front of St. John's Church in Washington, DC the day after thugs tried to burn it down. The pictures show him holding it correctly, but I remember hearing about this lie in 2021 from a liberal friend of mine from the People's Convoy. The amount of lies told about President Trump were preposterous, yet, he soldiered on "Like a Boss!"

I remember the debates and how they only had two, the first being extremely combative, while Trump backed off a bit but not enough to look weak in the second debate. I also remember the fly that rested on Mike Pence's head for about five minutes during the debate with Kamala Harris. I couldn't take my eyes off that pesky little thing. I remember just staring at it and laughing while talking to myself, probably under the influence of my whiskey. In the second presidential debate, Trump hit Biden with some allegations regarding payoffs from Russia, China, and Ukraine, which now are known to be true facts but were all deflected by the "impartial" moderator, Kristen Welker. I remember when Trump brought up the Logan Act from the first presidential debate and how Trump outed Biden as the mastermind behind the ousting of Lieutenant General (LTG) Mike Flynn. The look on Biden's face was priceless. It was as if he was caught with his hand in the cookie jar. Trump brought up a lot regarding what happened after he won his election in 2016. He said he caught them all. Was he foreshadowing things to come? I sure as heck never realized back then, but looking back on the last three years and how things have played out, I see how he was setting things up.

As I looked at the news reports from Fox (I couldn't stand any of the other news networks because of their constant propaganda), it was crystal clear to me there was no way on God's green Earth that Joe Biden was going to beat Teflon Don. He was just too weak of a candidate, propped up by the Mockingbird Media. I'll talk more about that later. I remember in one of Joe's appearances, former President Obama called Joe Biden to the stage, and there was no Joe to be found. He called on Joe numerous times until he was shown running to him. There was no way Joe would be president. The only way was a comprehensive plan to commit election fraud, which, by the way, Joe was seen on camera admitting to election fraud, not only for the 2020 election but the 2012 election as well. As they had done before, the media covered it up and gave some lame excuse, which some of the supporters actually believed.

On the second day of October, President Trump reported that he had contracted COVID-19. To this day, I am not sure if he had caught the virus or if this was some campaign strategy to give people more confidence so they were compelled to go out and vote. One of my colleagues at work who previously worked at the White House during the Bush Administration mentioned the possibility of Trump's enemies trying to take him out by placing a biological sample on something at one of the gatherings at the White House. I don't want to believe something such as this to be true, but it certainly is plausible and not too far-fetched from reality, as quite a few people caught COVID-19 a few days later.

Many people were still frightened and needed a strong leader to show that with the proper care, they could get through this. I was still fuming that the flu disappeared and people who died of heart attacks, car crashes, or falling off a building were considered as dying of COVID-19. This was complete and utter bollocks. I should have realized that if people could be fooled by going into a restaurant, taking their masks off at the table and putting them back on when they got up, they could be mind controlled into believing anything the media reported.

By October 5th, after various treatments at Walter Reed Army Medical Center, Trump returned to the White House. He was visibly winded after exiting Marine One and walked up the stairs to the second-floor balcony. He stopped, took off the mask, and saluted the flight crew. Whether he had it or not, the optics sure kept people guessing based on what looked like someone who'd just finished a two-mile run for a physical fitness test. Whether you liked him or not, he led by example and showed America there was no need to fear.

I don't remember exactly when I began following "Q," but I had known nothing about it for years. The first drops started in late October 2017, and I don't remember seeing anything about it since I didn't use Twitter. I mention this because many of the people I follow in the Truther movement were using Twitter to decode the Q drops. The only thing I remember before following was seeing pictures of this green frog named Pepe and wondering why he was called racist. I also remember my friend Lori posting some weird stuff on Facebook, and I would say to myself, "Man, I love Lori. She's a little crazy, but she's cool." Shout out to you, Lori! I realize now how crazy many of my friends and family may think I am after these years.

Dubbed 'Qanon' by the media and considered a cult, Qanon is a complete fabrication and PSYOP (psychological operation) driven by the mainstream media to drive people away from searching for the truth. It is widely believed by those in the Truth movement who follow the phenomenon that Q is a military operation designed to give the general public enough open-source intelligence to search and scour the internet and connect the dots without revealing highly classified information. Sometime right before the election, I stumbled onto the 8kun website, I can't explain how, and looked at the material. I'll be completely honest, I never understood what many of the Q intelligence drops meant, but I followed the experts with their explanations of what they meant and still do to this day. I remember seeing the introduction video by someone named Joe M, and I knew I wanted to be a part of this. The media constantly trashed 'Qanon,' but I never once heard them talking about Q. When Trump mentioned that the media was the enemy of the people, he truly meant it. I found this out on election night.

In early August, I signed up with Parler, a social media platform similar to Twitter. I don't remember how I found out about it, but it was probably from a segment on Fox News with Dan Bongino, since he was part owner of the platform and talked about it. I set up my account, followed a few people, spent some time on it, and then pretty much left it alone. Then, around the first part of October, there was a pretty big push to get more people on board. Immediately, Parler was dubbed by the elitists as a far-right platform, which, to me, was one of the most preposterous things I'd heard. One of the main reasons I couldn't stand watching mainstream media was that if you didn't fall for the narrative, you were placed in a class of misfits and deplorables. So, if you went in a different direction with your beliefs, you were coined as an extremist. This is all such a crock of you-know-what and a form of mind control the media has mastered for decades.

I found myself spending a lot of time on Parler. I mean, what else was I going to do with my time, right? There was only so much information going on with news programming (which is what all of this nonsense was - programming). There wasn't much going on with work, and I could only get so much information by watching the news or surfing the internet. What I found in Parler was a treasure trove of information. I would spend hours connecting and communicating with like-minded people from all over the world. This platform would be instrumental over the next couple of months in successfully leading me down the rabbit hole of The Great Awakening.

November 3rd had arrived, and I was excited for this day. For months, I had been following both campaigns and watched as Biden's campaign floundered while Trump's campaign was full of energy. I'd seen videos of people gathering in the streets, including in California, of massive amounts of people from all walks of life in support of the 45th President. I knew this election was a lock for four more years of winning. I only needed to wait for the polls to close and watch things play out with the so-called experts on television. Throughout the day, there were reports of inconsistencies with voting in certain areas. I wasn't worried, though, as I felt the atmosphere was all Trump.

Hawaii was five hours behind Washington D.C., so when the polls closed at 7:00 pm, it was 2:00 pm local time. Results started coming in, and things seemed pretty normal. One thing that I can't get wrapped around my head to this day, however, is how the media can call some races immediately after the polls close when there is not enough data to support calling it. Virginia, for example, was called for Biden immediately, yet less than 1 percent of the vote had been tallied. The television screen literally only showed a few hundred votes in a highly populated state.

As the night progressed, it was looking like a rout, with President Trump sailing into a second term. I monitored Parler and switched the television channels to all of the news organizations to see what each reported and how they reported things. Things were going extraordinarily well for Trump fans with his lead in some states, especially the swing states of Pennsylvania, Michigan, and Wisconsin. He had about a 700,000 vote lead in Pennsylvania, with almost ¾ of the vote tallied. About this time, I remember Mark Levin sending out a message over Parler asking why no one was calling the races in Pennsylvania, Georgia, Michigan, Wisconsin, and North Carolina. After all, the media was quick to call a state for Biden when he won, but why were they slow-walking things for Trump?

Fox later reported that Arizona voters were having problems at the polling stations. Apparently, poll workers were providing Arizonians with black Sharpie markers, instead of pens. Why would they do something like this? Using a Sharpie pen on paper bleeds through the paper, making the vote invalid because the electronic voting machine is unable to read who the vote was meant for properly. All of the major media organizations called this misinformation; however, this is a complete fabrication. The fact of the matter is that the voter is specifically instructed that the machine cannot properly read the voting card if there are marks outside of the bubble and to mark inside the lines carefully. Using a Sharpie will automatically bleed through. This has been proven by experts, but the Big Tech Censor Machine has kept this information from people who do not question the narrative. Despite reports of votes not counting in Arizona due to Sharpie Gate and a few other reports of voting irregularities around the country, Trump was still on his way to a major landslide victory. And then, the unthinkable happened.

With many votes to still be counted, the analysts at Fox called Arizona for Biden. "Was this a joke?" I thought. Arizona, from what I can remember, had always voted Red. Always! All of a sudden, it's Blue? I turned the channel to see what the other news organizations said. Not one other major news outlet called Arizona for Biden. I turned back to Fox, and I knew something was afoot. Brett Baier brought one of the analysts for Arizona on the air, Chris Stirewalt, and drilled him for information on why the team had called this race with so many more votes to count. Looking at Stirewalt's body language, I could tell he was nervous. I'd seen him on panels before, giving his insight, and I agreed with much of his analysis. But on this night, he was visibly nervous about something, and I could see right through it. It almost looked as if he was sweating while giving his insight to millions of people watching. He did such a bad con job his boss had to take over and explain how the team came up with their decision to call Arizona so early in the night. What I saw in Stirewalt's boss was a masterful liar, but those of us who question the narrative saw right through it. Funny enough, Fox fired Stirewalt a couple of months later after working there for years.

After Arizona, everything went downhill. For the first time in our nation's history, vote counting on election night completely stopped. There were reports of flooding in Georgia, which later turned out to be a leaking toilet. Why in the world did the counting need to be stopped? Reports came in that they would stop counting the vote and start again the next morning. This was an unprecedented move never done before in the history of our Republic. And when the counting stopped, and the majority (not all) of the vote counters left, the steal began. The aftermath of what happened on November 3rd and the middle of the night on the 4th will truly live in infamy in the American historical landscape.

Chapter 4

Election Aftermath

I woke up in complete shock the morning of November 4th when checking the news; I found out that all of Trump's major leads had completely disappeared. I couldn't understand what had happened. When I went to bed, the president was well ahead and on the road to a smashing victory against Vice President Biden. I couldn't understand why the monstrous leads in Pennsylvania, Georgia, Wisconsin, and Michigan had all vanished. Most of the vote tally was in when I went to bed the night before, and ballot counting had stopped. I couldn't believe what I was seeing. I immediately signed in to the Parler App on my iPad to see what was happening.

All I could see were posts of people saying there was election fraud. The election wasn't over yet, but Biden apparently had a clear lead. What in the hell happened overnight? The last thing I remembered before going to bed was President Trump in a commanding lead, even though counting had stopped in numerous states. But why? Why in the world would counting be stopped? Never in the history of our country had vote counting been stopped on election night. I wondered why Trump was conducting a press conference calling for the counting to cease. I thought that was very odd since he was ahead by so much the night before. I was totally flabbergasted seeing this at that moment.

As I checked further into Parler, stories and videos were popping up all over showing the cheat. I looked at Fox, and to my horror, they, too, were playing along with Biden running ahead to a very strong lead. This is when I realized the fix was in. But how deep was it? I mean, Fox News wouldn't be a part of this? There's no way this was happening! This couldn't happen in the United States of America, the land of the free and the home of the brave! I quickly learned that Fox News called Arizona early for Biden after the report of issues at Arizona polling stations, followed by the shutting down of vote counting across the major battleground states in the country. Arizona was the trigger point for all of the election interference to follow. Treason! A complete takeover of my beloved country and a massive and coordinated cover up - a Coup de' tat.

I was mortified! I immediately stopped watching Fox News and searched for anything I could find. Many of the folks on Parler mentioned that Newsmax was reporting that things weren't right. I had downloaded the Newsmax app to watch on my television a couple of weeks prior, but I hadn't really tuned in at this point. So I went on and began watching. After seeing Fox do what they did as their part in this rigged and stolen election, I would never pay homage to that station again.

News reports began to pour in on Newsmax. No other station was showing what Newsmax was showing, with the exception of One America News (OAN). I hadn't watched that channel at this point and stayed with Newsmax to get my up-to-date coverage. November 4th was my day at the office, and I went in about 30 minutes later than usual, which was okay since there were just a couple of us there, and it was still before the military personnel arrived. I worked most days with Dan, our deputy, since the command team alternated days.

I remember walking into his office and saying, "Hello, Comrade! (I mentioned 'Comrade' to signify the Communist takeover of America) Can you believe what the hell happened? Trump was winning by so much. I don't understand what's going on, but he won last night. I know he did."

Dan agreed with me that something was afoot with the night before. But at our levels, there was nothing that either one of us could do about it. Hank Holiday, our civilian counterpart with the Inspections Branch, was also working that day. He couldn't believe it either. So all three of us gathered and talked about what happened for most of the morning, wondering what

President Trump would do because he was furious. My morale had immediately sunk since if what we all thought was true, there was an illegal takeover of the United States Government, something none of us could have ever imagined. And for whatever reason, the CIG was in that day, maybe since Wednesdays were staff briefings. I was wearing a blue shirt that day. He looked at it and said, "Mike, are you Red or Blue?"

I looked him in the eye and said, "I'm Red, White, and Blue, Sir!"

He nodded his head and said, "Good."

From this point forward, I was glued to my television set and Parler when I was at home. I went on Facebook as well and started dropping bombs. I saw video footage of Republican pollsters kicked out of the polling stations while Democrats placed large pieces of thick paper or cardboard on the polling station windows. Video evidence continually showed up on election night coverage, where Trump would have a certain number of votes, but the next time the information showed up on the screen, it would show a number of votes less from the last time. Still, that same amount subtracted from Trump's total, was added to Biden's. There were videotapes showing time stamps of the middle of the night when vans showed up at polling stations, and people were taking suitcases out. Inside these suitcases were ballots. Why were they showing up now? Everyone was sent home hours before this, and there were all kinds of video evidence showing all of these places bringing in vans filled with suitcases or other types of cases loaded with illegal ballots.

In Georgia, after everyone was sent home, video footage showed several individuals pulling cases out from underneath the tables. These cases were filled with ballots. These people, without any proper supervision, were putting these ballots through the card readers. They would put these same ballots through a few times. Newsmax reported this, yet none of the other networks, including Fox, touched it. When I found this information, I posted it on Facebook. It wasn't long before I was censored for trying to spread the truth. This steal was *massive!* Everyone was involved; the Democrats, the Republicans, media, big tech, Hollywood, and some of our foreign allies and adversaries around the globe.

Those of us who realized what the hell happened were shouting from the rooftops, but no one seemed to listen. I was all over Facebook calling out treason, and it seemed like the only ones who agreed with me were along conservative lines. My friend Nav called me from Korea, though, I think the day before the election was called for Biden, on November 6th. Nav let me know that I shouldn't feel alone. He had a friend visiting from Guam or Japan, and we talked about it. If I remember correctly, Nav's friend's name was Steve. I haven't talked with Nav in a while because, well, given the fact this fight has been so deep and dark, I've disconnected myself from most of my liberal friends.

I didn't want to, but I had received some vitriol and

felt it better to go my own way. I truly hope I can reconnect with Nav and Luanna in the near future. But I digress. I talked with his friend, who wholeheartedly agreed with me that this election was a complete fraud. The media kept reporting that this was the most secure election in history, but that was a complete fabrication of the facts. I couldn't understand how people couldn't see this. I talked with his friend about this for a while, and I know Nav knew as well, but I understand the world he lives in because I lived it with him. We normally didn't discuss politics, and that made us better friends because of it. I spoke with him quite a few times after this point, but after I left Hawaii, the last thing I did for Nav was a birthday video from the hotel room I lived in that Luanna set up. I just finished a job I'd worked at for six weeks and was in over my head. I completed the video, drunk, and wished him a happy birthday. This was in February 2022, and we have not connected since.

Talking with Nav and Luanna was one of my bright spots after leaving Korea. I became very close with those two, especially Nav, over the years, since we met when I was stationed in Seoul for my last tour of duty in uniform with the Army. They both were very understanding of what I was going through with this loss. I want the reader to understand that I didn't give a damn that Trump 'lost.' What I cared about was an obvious overthrow of a duly elected American president, and yet, no one seemed to care. I mean, did people hate

Trump enough not to care that he was removed illegally? I felt a strong sense of betrayal from my countrymen, whom I swore an oath to protect. For twenty-one years, I, and many others like me, put our lives on the line to protect our nation, yet this moment to me was worse than soldiers being spit on after coming home from Vietnam.

I called my wife and spoke to her numerous times regarding the election theft. In 2020, we had been married for 26 years. I met her in Nuremberg, Germany, in 1993. She was an East German living in Rostock at the time of the collapse of the Soviet Union. I provided a life for her. Yet, she rolled her eyes and scoffed at me when I said that many people in positions of power committed treason. I felt like she didn't care. I heard her bring up the fact that the Founders of our Constitution were slaveholders. The Constitution be damned! I was shocked at hearing all of this when I saw my country was under attack. I didn't know who this woman was anymore. We'd been growing apart for years, but COVID-19 and the stolen election completely deteriorated what was left of our marriage in my eyes. I couldn't even get her to agree to visit me during the plandemic because she didn't want to stay quarantined in my apartment for two weeks. It didn't matter that I hadn't seen her since more than 12 months prior, and our average visits were once every 12-18 months over the past decade. By now, I was done. It was just a matter of time before I would pull the plug on our relationship.

I continued on Parler and Newsmax. Story after story on Newsmax talked about election fraud. Evidence piled up between Parler and Newsmax. I was mortified that no one seemed to be listening. Hearings were conducted in many swing states such as Georgia, Michigan, Arizona, and Pennsylvania. Hundreds came forward, signed affidavits, and testified before these committees. Countless pieces of evidence were presented, much of it video evidence. Press conferences were held almost daily by President Trump, his staff, and lawyers. Nobody was listening. I couldn't believe this information was not getting out to the public.

This continued until Inauguration Day, January 20th. No matter what information came forward, the media would say it was disinformation or conspiracy theories. The controlled media narrative was that "the 2020 election was the most secure election in history." This was a bald-faced lie pushed by almost everyone, save the ones who shouted from the rooftops that this was a fraud and an assault on the United States Republic. I thought going through COVID was rough, but this would be the beginning of my roller coaster ride through the hell I could see before me. From here, I would venture into the rabbit hole.

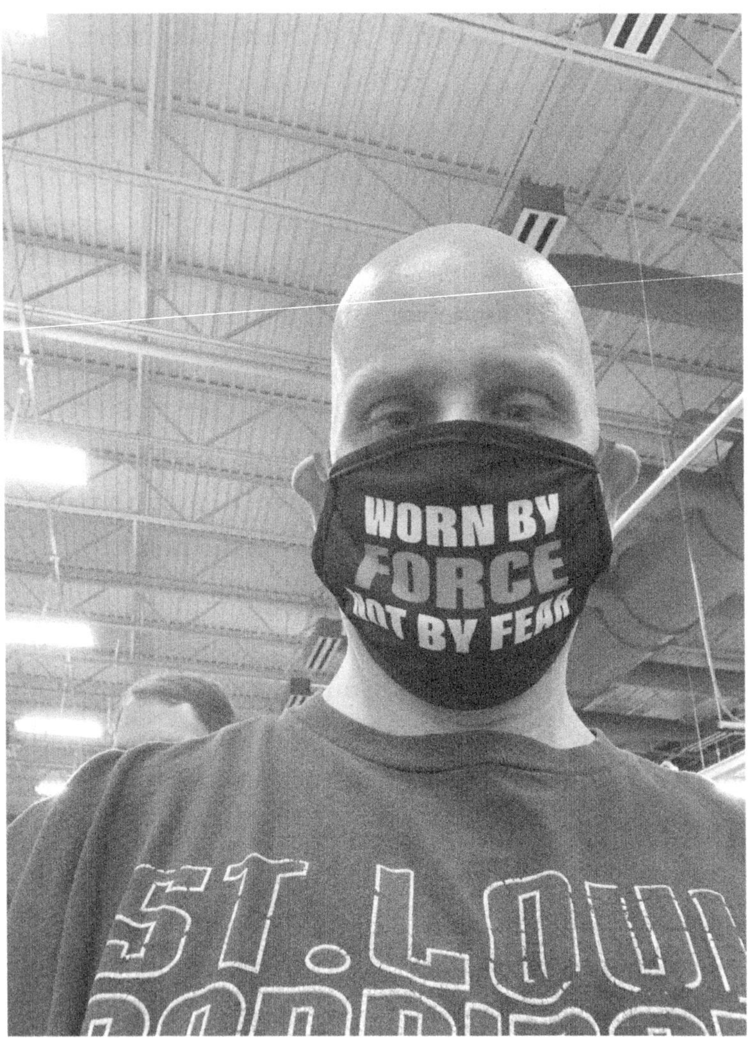
WORN BY
FORCE
NOT BY FEAR

Chapter 5

Down the Rabbit Hole

After the election steal, I found myself venturing down the rabbit hole of truth. There was a *massive* amount of information flowing across Parler. Not only was I finding countless stories and videos regarding November 3rd, but I was also stumbling across knowledge that would tear at my fabric as a human being. This was the beginning of many phases of cognitive dissonance I would experience. I cannot say exactly where I found all of the information because when I stumbled upon something, sometimes it led me to something totally different. Everything I stumbled onto, however, I believe, was by design. Between the different topics I found on Parler, to certain articles or links friends would send me, to just accidentally falling into something mysteriously, I felt the Hand of God giving me enlightenment on what was going on around me and the rest of the world. I was finally seeing things that had long been hidden in plain sight. I was always 'awake' per se, but there were certain aspects I had never seen before that would allow me to connect the dots in a way which never before seemed plausible.

Around the time after the election, I stumbled across a podcast called The Health Ranger Report, hosted by Mike Adams. Mike Adams, I learned, was a scientist. I began listening to his podcast every morning. The election hit me extremely hard, and I began drinking a lot more because of it. By now, I had gone into my freezer at lunchtime on many days to retrieve the whiskey I had stored there. Every morning while at home, it became a ritual to listen to this podcast. It later became normal for me to listen to different podcasts during the day so I could immerse myself in the information on what was *really* happening in my world. But Mike Adams, at this point in time, was instrumental in my views of coronavirus and the looming rollout of the COVID-19 vaccine that was about to be unleashed on the world.

To the untrained eye, Mike Adams was nothing more than a conspiracy theorist, spreading dangerous disinformation to the public. But as I ventured on and listened to many others who were saying the same things, along with my own doubt about the COVID-19 narrative, I quickly learned I needed to listen closely to what this man was saying. It was through Mike and many others that I quickly learned about the true nature of the New World Order. The New World Order was nothing less than Satanism, designed to depopulate and enslave the world through clandestine means. I learned that all of the organizations and people we trust have sold us out. This is what President Trump opened our eyes to. George HW Bush called for the New World Order thirty years before, and the 2020 election was the trigger that allowed the Deep State to usher totalitarianism into the world at full throttle.

I learned that Bill Gates and organizations such as the World Economic Forum, the World Health Organization, The United Nations, NATO, the European Union, the Center For Disease Control and Prevention (CDC), Dr. Fauci, and others were in lockstep with the rollout of these vaccines worldwide. I learned quickly that this connected Cabal was the Fourth Reich, waging war on all of the people of the world. This was the One World fascist government ushering in the Nazi World Order with the spread of propaganda through the media and with the censorship of Big Tech. This was planned and rehearsed over a very long time with sharp precision, and it was very effective in casting a spell on much of humanity. Event 201 at Johns Hopkins University was the preparation by the Nazi World Order to unleash war on humanity.

I first learned the term Fourth Reich from Mel K, who previously worked with Donald Trump a few years prior to his presidency at Mar-a-lago in Florida. Mel claimed President Trump knew her by name, which I verified later when he gave a speech to a room full of women at an event in Florida when I heard him greet her as "Melody." Through Mel and human rights attorney Leigh Dundas, I quickly learned that though America defeated the Germans in WWII, they did not defeat the Nazi Party. In fact, many high-ranking Nazi scientists were brought to the United States at the end of the war. This operation was known as Operation Paperclip. Operation Paperclip is well-known to those of us with opened eyes, and those who don't know about it will be well-informed once they research it.

I remember a text conversation I had early on with my Aunt Diana. When I mentioned I thought all of these people were part of a rising Fourth Reich and hit send, my phone began doing strange things, such as scribbling in the text box. I could not send anything to my aunt. The Big Tech algorithms caught on to the Fourth Reich and went into action. My aunt immediately texted me to continue the conversation on Signal. Signal was an app that we talked on because it was supposed to be secure. I didn't believe this because I felt that everything was being monitored, but it was a way for people to feel as if they were communicating securely. My aunt confirmed that she had seen the same thing happen on her phone. I think this was the moment I realized that this war had many levels.

We, as a people, were silently and unwittingly thrust into World War III by our own governments and these organizations I mentioned above, who were not elected by the people of the world. No, WWIII would not be a thermonuclear war like we had been programmed to think. WWIII is a war, unlike any war we have faced in human history. This war is spiritual, psychological, biological, informational, clandestine, and kinetic rolled up into one. This would be the war to end all wars, and it would be waged by God and the devil with all of us together as pieces on the chess board.

During this time, I dove further into the Q operation. Most of the time, when I looked at the intelligence "drops" of Q, I couldn't understand what was going on with this. However, over time, I would at least have a better understanding that during this war on humanity, Q, with the help of smart folks who could interpret the different multiple meanings of these drops, was a multi-year operation with several layers designed to defeat those who want to destroy us through psychological operations and other means. The first real training I remember was a video produced by someone known as Joe M, who I'd found on Parler. His video, titled *Q: The Plan To Save the World,* is a video a little more than 13 minutes in length that details the elites and their cabal with insidious plans to wage war on humanity and to depopulate and enslave the world. This sounds completely crazy, I know, but this war is a war for "all the marbles," as Juan O. Savin says.

The video starts with, "Do you ever wonder why we go to war?" It is a very powerful narration explaining that people we trusted the most to lead and influence us such as politicians, news media, entertainers, etc., did not have our best interests in mind. It stated that the criminals infiltrated and achieved positions high up in government, news, entertainment, and banking. I was given an education that showed me that all of the US presidents after President Reagan were members of this conspiracy and that they would partner up with other criminals within their web around the world. It was explained that high-ranking military officials were aware of the cabal and considered attempting to remove President Barack Obama but ultimately did not pursue this course of action because the American people would not be open to this in a democratic Republic. As the story continues, this is when they approached Trump to run for president. Q, it said, was a military intelligence operation designed to give the masses hints through what were called "breadcrumbs" to assist researchers with information about this silent war to awaken those who are asleep and take down the cabal once and for all.

As crazy as this sounds, this was just the tip of the iceberg. Through this journey, I have stumbled on some of the most insane truths known to us. At this moment in time, there were things I *could not* watch. I learned something new and dark on an almost daily basis. It made me queasy how unrealistic some of this stuff was, and some things I could not wrap my head around. I felt as if nearly everything we were taught we were going to have to unlearn. I wasn't ready for all of this coming from a firehose, but I didn't have a say in the matter. I quickly learned that God wanted me to know all of these truths I had difficulty seeing, and if you have difficulty believing God is real, I can tell you, without a shadow of a doubt, that He is real! And He woke me up to what has been going on behind the veil for a reason. I don't know where this journey ends in writing this book at this point in time. I'm not sure how deep this book will go. I can assure you all, however, that I am writing my story of the last four years through Him. So, I fully expect this story to take a life of its own.

During November and December 2020, I found evidence through Parler and different podcasters I watched that the Presidential election of 2020 was a sting operation by Trump and the "White Hats." The White Hats, I learned, were the Patriots fighting against the "Black Hats" of the Deep State. They were a part of the Q Operational plan. Information surfaced that President Trump and select members of his team were located in the Sensitive Compartmented Information Facility (SCIF) of the Eisenhower Executive Office Building across from the West Wing of the White House on election night, monitoring information that showed election interference not only from foreign entities but also interference on the domestic homefront. I also learned from a friend in DoD I worked with overseas that the sting operation was in play. Information later surfaced that the Space Force, created in 2019, monitored the election data worldwide and stored that data in real-time. They caught all the actors who conspired against our nation, both foreign and domestic.

There were days that I literally couldn't get out of bed. My depression and anxiety continued to take hold. I couldn't sleep. I began to put on extra weight due to my eating habits. The gyms were open again, but masks were required, and I was no longer able to breathe properly while conducting exercise on cardio equipment. Unlike the last time I was at the gym, I couldn't get properly motivated and was completely out of shape. My morale was shot, which I think was one of the objectives because it tore me down physically, mentally, emotionally, and spiritually. My inside battle was raging on all fronts, and to add insult to injury, I was completely alone; literally, I was stranded on an island without family or friends. This awakening was the loneliest I had ever experienced in almost fifty years. Thank God for awakened friends and my Aunt Diana because I'm not sure I would be here today without them. Of course, I can't leave God out of this equation. Between the subtle hints that He was right next to me and those few I shared this journey with at the time, I have since broken free of the chains that bound me, though it was not easy by any means.

Back in late 2020, after feeling a range of emotions, after bawling my eyes out at what happened to our country in the dead of night, I was confident that before January, Trump and his team would act. All of the information that was put forth regarding the steal would bring forth arrests on a scale never seen. I remember watching a video on YouTube with human rights attorney Leigh Dundas regarding President Trump's Executive Order (EO) 13848 - Imposing Certain Sanctions in the Event of Foreign Interference in a United States Election, dated September 12, 2018. Ms. Dundas gave a fabulous tutorial on how those caught with election theft would forfeit rights to everything they own. This covered domestic assets owned by US citizens, but it also covered assets owned within the US borders by foreign entities. Between witnessing all of the theft and cheating during the 2020 election, I knew that President Trump had something up his sleeve that we would find out about before January 20th.

I continued down the rabbit hole and stumbled across Juan O. Savin. Juan was an interesting individual, as when he interviewed, he would never show his face. Most of the interviews were conducted in hotel rooms, showing only his boot, the ruby ring he wears on his right pinky finger, and the opposite wall. Juan was long-winded, so you had to have the patience to listen to him, but the information he gave was highly interesting and entertaining. I loved hearing the story of Osiris and how Juan tied that story in with the Washington Monument and similar monuments around the world.

Many in the Truth Movement cannot listen to Juan since he is very wordy, but I listen to him when I can, and I was given a chance to meet him later on. I felt truly blessed and comforted because there was a series of events that happened that allowed me to be in this place and time with him, but I will address that piece in a later chapter. If you haven't had a chance to listen to him, he teamed up with his wife, Jennifer, to make a movie titled *"The Called: The Makings For a Perfect Day."* You can find it on YouTube and Rumble. If you are sour about what happened during the election, this is an interesting watch. I've watched it numerous times, and pick up something new every time because it is all about the numbers.

I can go on and on about things I found. The deeper I went, the more unrealistic and dark it became. Volumes can be written about what I found, what was believable and what was truly insane. But this particular story is not about that. This story is about my continuous struggle of finding light in the darkness, the roller coaster ride from hell that Jesus sat next to me on. I struggled with my demons and ultimately overcame them. It wasn't easy, but He was there every step of the way to guide me. And though this battle is not completely over, I can see the light ahead, and He has given me the foresight to put my experiences to print. Everything is connected through the numbers, and we just need to connect the dots. And while I will be the first one to admit that I don't know what the numbers are about completely, and I'm still a bit confused with Gematria, I can say without a doubt, it all adds up in the end. I am stoked about the future because, in the end, GOD WINS!

Chapter 6

The "Insurrection" and Inauguration

At the end of December, I was hopeful that the traitors would all be arrested and brought to justice. There were battles going on all fronts to get Trump to stay in the White House. The engine was firing on all cylinders, with Mayor Guliani spearheading hearings in the state legislatures regarding the election fraud, the state of Texas bringing suit with numerous other states to the Supreme Court, retired Air Force Lieutenant General McInerny giving interviews about the CIA *Hammer* and *Scorecard*, which helped them overthrow governments in the past, countless evidence showing involvement by MI-5, MI-6, Italy, Germany, and other allies interfering in the 2020 election through cyber attacks. So much evidence was out there showing how the election was stolen from the American people. And yet, the censorship on a global scale was immense. There were dozens of court cases regarding the steal presented to the courts, but most were thrown out over lack of "standing." The courts didn't want to touch this, and none of us could understand why. Unless the corruption was so deep that everything in our system of government had been infiltrated. Q was right. The military would be the only way.

But how would this happen? Would they go in and make mass arrests? Who would they target beyond the obvious? The evidence we saw come in was heavy, massive, and widespread. What were they going to do? We all were waiting anxiously, as we knew the stakes were high. Communists had infiltrated the government and taken over the country, for God's sake, and we wanted our country back, NOW! Were we about to witness the ten days of darkness, as stated in the Q drops? The wait was excruciating, and I continued to have a full range of emotions while alone in my apartment. There were times I just bawled at what I saw happen to the country I raised my right hand to defend. I wanted to do something, but I couldn't figure out what to do for the life of me. I was helpless. The only thing I could do was spread the word over Facebook, and that I did. To those who had no idea the election was stolen (I still can't figure that part out), I must have looked like a stark, raving lunatic. But I was now on a mission to spread the word and let the people know what happened shouldn't have come to pass. My censorship over Facebook was beginning, and I would come to have a very long list of Facebook crimes that kept me in a restricted status for most of the rest of the time until now.

I continued to plead with my wife over Facetime, phone, and text, but it didn't take hold. It was almost as if she was glad it happened. I gave reason after reason of how I felt traitors had taken over our government, and still, nothing from her. I felt betrayed, and it made me rethink our whole marriage because an enemy from within had taken everything away from us, and many were asleep to this, but my wife was too smart for this. She was too highly educated in the European school system to downplay everything I presented. We had been married for 26 years by now, and given our long term geographical separation, I was no longer feeling the love and patience for her anymore. My country and its existence were the fights I was ready to face, and I didn't need a critical thinker's lack of critical thinking to be in my corner. It was just a matter of time before I would pull the ripcord on our marriage.

January 6th was an interesting day for me. Hawaii doesn't change clocks like most of the rest of the US, and in winter, Hawaii is 5 hours behind the East Coast. I was scheduled to go to work that day but caught the president's speech in full before going in. The speech lasted over one hour, and President Trump laid out his case to the American people. No one knows the actual number of supporters in Washington, D.C., on that day, but according to some estimates, somewhere between 1-2 million people supported the 45th President. Trump talked about his insurmountable lead in many states at 10:00 pm, only to lose those leads during the dead of night, after the precincts stopped counting votes. He stated he hoped Vice President Pence would do the right thing.

I noticed during the speech he talked about Pence having the courage to do nothing. This happened during the first eight minutes of the speech, and it caught my ear. I wondered why he said that. It sounded like he was hoping Pence would not do the duty he was committed to under the Constitution and allow the state legislatures to decide since there were so many irregularities during the election. But why would Trump say it would be more courageous to do nothing in regard to the election? One theory mentions Continuity of Government (COG). More information on this theory can be found at devolution.link where Jon Herold, AKA Patel Patriot, argues that President Trump devolved the government while a secret war was waged worldwide. Jon put together a captivating twenty-five-part series explaining his belief. After witnessing all that has happened, a critical thinker can at least agree a theory such as this is plausible.

I went to work after the speech and scoured the internet on my phone when I could. Sometimes we would actually have work to do, so I wasn't always able to surf the web, but I remember on this day doing so in my office. I shared my office with one other person, but we rarely were in the office on the same day, so I was free to listen to things as long as the volume was down. By the late morning, I heard reports of protesters inside the Capitol. As with everything, first reports are sketchy because not all the smoke clears, per se. But by the end of the day, it was evident that one Trump supporter, Ashli Babbitt, an Air Force veteran, was killed by a Capitol Police officer inside. Others were killed as well, and their stories will be told, but this one, in particular, was the one that stuck out at first, since so much mayhem was going on.

Videos began coming out of what happened on January 6th the very next day. There were many telltale signs that this "insurrection" was not real, that it was a show with a narrative of Trump supporters storming in and taking over the United States Capitol. I learned about Ray Epps in the early days, speaking to crowds the night before and attempting to rile people up and go into the capitol the next day. The crowds began to shout him down and, at one point, shouted, "Fed! Fed! Fed!" These Patriots knew what was going on, and they did not want any part of it. There was more footage of Epps instigating people to go inside on January 6th, and this was just the tip of the iceberg. Evidence shows the Capitol Police moving bicycle racks out of the way and allowing people through. I was shown video evidence of no less than four buses being escorted in with people dressed all in black - Antifa! Thousands of hours of camera footage have never been released to the public from the mainstream media. Why is this? Because the fact that possibly 2 million people who showed up in support of President Trump against the Treason that happened on November 3rd didn't fall in line with the narrative, and the media was a part of the Treason as well.

Through my research, I was also aware that something else was in the mix that day. I saw footage from inside the Capitol of men dressed like Antifa carrying backpacks. They were seen moving down the steps expeditiously. The stairs and hallways were crowded with Trump supporters, who realized Antifa had earlier infiltrated them. They shouted at these men and looked as if they were about to apprehend them. One of them shouted, "We are not here to be Antifa." Over a dozen laptops were taken from inside the Capitol, including Speaker Pelosi's. The Q Shaman, later identified as Jacob Chansley (who I liked to call 'Viking Man') was shown going into the House chamber with an American flag. He addressed a Capitol police officer and assured him he would not do anything irrational inside. This video was released over the mainstream many moons later. What has yet to be released was the note he dropped in the place Speaker Pelosi sat when the US President addressed a joint session of Congress. In the video, he writes a note and calls her a traitor.

It can be said that Mr. Chansley was an Antifa infiltrator who had been seen earlier at an Antifa rally in Arizona dressed as he was on January 6th, but I have another theory. Jacob Chansley was formerly a member of the US Navy. Is it possible that what happened at the Capitol on January 6th was a distraction to conduct a military special operation to catch the traitors who were involved in the election theft? Looking at many hours of uncirculated footage of what happened that day, I find it very plausible that an operation of this type transpired. It's common knowledge in some circles that the US Special Forces infiltrated Antifa and BLM long before January 6th. I also learned that Jacob Chansley was a Naval Intelligence Officer. Given what happened throughout 2020 and culminating with the events that happened on January 6th, if America was truly at war, and with the election theft, I believe we are, one should ask, could it not be plausible that President Trump ordered a military operation to save our Republic?

In the future, I hope to hear the real story of what went on that day because documented evidence shows the infiltration of Antifa amongst the Trump supporters, who, very well, could have held the US Capitol under siege with their numbers that day if they wanted to. They didn't, though, because that was not what their goal was on that day. The goal was to show everyone that they knew the vote was rigged, and they were there to show their support. They wanted to see the President of the Senate do the job he was supposed to do because of the many voting irregularities that happened on the night of November 3rd and subsequent days afterward.

I want to jump topics a bit here because I think it is important to note that this war is multifaceted. So, you'll notice at times, I may jump around a bit, but I want you to realize that there was so much going on with me in my life, as I was taking all of this information every day while living in solitude. I want to keep things in chronological order as best I can, but sometimes I will cross over to information I was given. Why am I saying this right now? I am saying this because I believe, *and I know,* this walk I take is a walk with God. I know the information I received was real, and I had to learn very quickly how to discern reality from fantasy along this journey.

Around the same time this happened, in early January, I remember the time I decided to work out at Planet Fitness. As I have said before, my morale was shot from everything that happened in the previous year. It only took a short time to break down physically and mentally from what happened around us, and being alone during these times was the worst possible prison sentence one could have. As I write this, I think about those at the end of their lives who could not see their loved ones because of the fear mongering from the people in positions of power. What hell those poor people were put through is beyond anything many of us could imagine.

I arrived at the Ala Moana Mall Parking Garage across the street from Planet Fitness and parked on the ground level like I always had before. It had been a while since I worked out at the gym, and this was the first time I had come since they re-opened in November

2020. The second I exited my car, I felt something wasn't right. I looked around to see four or five people walking around with their masks on outside, as if they were zombies. It was quite surreal to witness their actions moving in slow motion. As I watched this, a white Cadillac Escalade with red rims and lights underneath was slowly driving through the garage; windows opened with hypnotic music blaring for all to hear. I immediately felt different, euphoric, I would describe it. It was almost intoxicating in the way I started feeling dizzy suddenly. I walked across the street to wait my turn before entering Planet Fitness. I opened the Planet Fitness app on my phone to be ready to place the phone on the reader at the front desk. While looking at the page, I noticed gears being turned towards each other. I then immediately looked up, decided today was not a good day to work out and made a beeline directly for my car.

I was freaked out because what came over me was not good. I felt a shroud of darkness trying to take hold of me. It was as if I was in two worlds at once, and I knew if I didn't leave immediately, this spell I could feel being cast would engulf me like the zombies had been engulfed. I left and drove in a different direction than I normally drove when I finished my workouts. Since I was isolated for the past year, I was unfamiliar with the downtown area. I was worried at first about getting lost, but God assured me He was with me and would guide me. I drove for about 5 minutes or so and found the entrance to the freeway without making one wrong turn. I will never forget that day because the evil I felt trying to place me in a trance could no longer penetrate my spirit. Folks, this Spiritual War is real whether you realize it or not. Some of us are completely in tune to it, while others have fallen into that trance. I believe it is our duty to wake these people up, and God is using us to do just that.

As January 20th was approaching quickly, rumors were swelling across the Truther community that arrests would be made during the inauguration of Biden. Many of us were becoming uneasy about the prospects because we thought the "steal" would be stopped long before now. I was confident by now that the election was indeed a sting operation and that Trump would act decisively and soon, as we were running out of time. I remember watching a podcast between Juan O. Savin and Michael Jaco, a former Navy S.E.A.L. and CIA operative, where Juan gave a scenario of Biden being sworn in and becoming the 46th President of the United States. I was mortified because I knew exactly what that would mean. It meant darkness would lie ahead. Juan stated that America would need to face a 'near-death' experience and reach the precipice before being brought back from that ledge of destruction.

On the morning of January 20, 2021, President Trump addressed a crowd of supporters at Joint Base Andrews, with the steps to Air Force One behind him. He made it clear earlier that he would not be seated in the crowd during the Biden inauguration and left Washington D.C. that morning. There were two items he talked about that particularly grabbed my attention. He stated his administration was not a regular administration and that he would be back in some form. What exactly did he mean by that? As I have learned, President Trump was a part of the Q operation, and Continuity of Government, or Devolution, was a very plausible theory.

As the morning went on, it became clear that Joe Biden would be sworn in as the 46th President. Many of us were holding out hope that there would be a very large amount of arrests made on live television since the military had a huge presence in the Capital. None of this was to transpire, however, as Joseph Robinette Biden Jr. was sworn in as President at 11:47 am in direct violation of the Twentieth Amendment to the Constitution. For thirteen minutes on January 20, 2021, America had two presidents since, technically, the president is to be sworn into office at noon that day, per the Twentieth Amendment to the Constitution. The very first act of this illegitimate regime was to violate the Law of the Land, thus ushering in the criminal organization that would be the end of America and the rise of the 4th Reich, known as The New World Order.

Chapter 7

Turning the Page

After the inauguration passed without Trump sliding back into the Oval Office for a second term, I hit rock bottom. All of the evidence that was presented from state legislature hearings, the hundreds of sworn affidavits from ordinary law-abiding citizens, and video tapings of crimes committed between November 3rd and January 6th went nowhere. This election was the 'most secure election in our nation's history,' they told us. Our country was lost. I went into a deep depression, and though I knew in my heart of hearts Trump would not abandon his post after witnessing first hand the treason that befell our nation, I still could not understand why we were subject to this blatant lie.

Thank God I only needed to go into the office one day a week. That one day was difficult enough to get up out of my bed, take a shower, and get ready for work. I would check my social media daily just to see if there was a change in the situation, and every day, nothing changed. I didn't want to face anyone in the office except for Dan and Hank, so when they were not at work I pretty much hid in my office, hoping that I would be left alone. The rest of the week, I stayed on my couch, where I slept every night. Many mornings, I was hungover from drinking half a bottle of whiskey from the night before. I always checked my government laptop, located on a television tray in front of the couch, to see if there were any important emails to deal with, but 95 percent of the time there was nothing awaiting me. There were many mornings the blanket covered my head completely, as I did not want to face the world. Sometimes, on days I wasn't hungover from the night before, I started drinking whiskey around noon. I would drink maybe two glasses to catch a buzz and leave it alone until 4:30 pm when the day was over. It would not have gone well if anyone called me in the afternoon with anything important. This went on until around the end of February when things began to turn around personally for me.

Sometime during the end of February, around my birthday, while checking for job openings in Korea, I found a job announcement for Inspector General at 8th United States Army Headquarters. I was not sure I wanted to leave Korea for Hawaii in the first place, and this was my chance to return. I applied for the position and was interviewed by telephone a couple of weeks later. I knew all three panel members, one of whom was my former deputy from down south in Daegu. I don't always conduct interviews well, but on this occasion, I felt very comfortable, given my advanced knowledge of the IG system by this time and the fact that I was comfortable interviewing since we all knew each other well. They all had known me for years and were very familiar with the products I produced. Within a few days, I received notice that 8th Army wanted to enlist my services, and I was given a tentative offer to live and work in Korea once more.

At this point, I needed to make a choice about my marriage. My wife, at this point, I felt, gave me zero support, even to the point where she told me I should seek counseling from a therapist. Granted, with everything I had been through over the years, it probably wasn't a bad idea. However, most of the medical community pushed the vaccine I so vehemently opposed. I didn't trust talking about my problems to community members who, by and large, I considered not to be in tune with what happened to our country on November 3rd. I wanted to go to Korea for a fresh start. So I decided it was time to cut ties with her, and I asked her for a divorce. Before I go into this, I think it's important to give context to Korea and a back story, because even today, this subject is in play.

Before leaving Korea in November 2019, I was involved in an extramarital affair. It began in late July of that year when I went out for dinner with my Korean landlord. I didn't know it then, but she planned on picking up a friend to join us. Her friend's name was MinKyoung. We ate at this sushi place in Daegu called Snow Pea, which I had frequented a few times before. We had a great time and had terrific chemistry. She was married and was a Pilates instructor with her own studio in town. At the time, I had lost 40 pounds over the previous six months and was the most fit I had been in 25 years. After dinner, I asked my landlord to call and schedule an appointment to learn Pilates. At this point, the thought of an affair never crossed my mind. I had a nice time at dinner and was interested in learning more about Pilates, since I heard it was a real ball-buster and hadn't done it before. We set up an appointment for Saturday, two days later.

I arrived on Saturday at her studio, and we had a session. I was in great shape then, and though doing Pilates hurt, especially the breathing techniques, Min was pretty impressed with my ability to handle it. When the session was complete, we agreed on a number of sessions - I think it was five - and I paid her in advance for them. I wasn't thinking of anything out of the ordinary at this point. I just thought she was a nice person who kicked my butt at Pilates.

On Monday evening, she called me and asked if I wanted to go to one of the mountains in Daegu the next day. I liked to hike, but I hadn't been to this particular mountain, and I always loved having company since I was a loner most of the time in Daegu. I had expatriate friends up in Seoul that I would go visit on long weekends, but that wasn't always enough for me. I knew, however, this was a bit different. I didn't know where this would go, but at this point, I was willing to see.

Tuesday afternoon, we met at a mutually agreed parking lot, and I opted to drive. On the drive, we talked about our families. I told her that I'd been married for 25 years at the time, but many years of my marriage I had spent alone. I don't know why I was telling her this, but I just felt comfortable doing so. Her story was very similar to mine. She was married for 20 years and had two teenage boys, one who was about to go into compulsory service with the Korean Army and the other who was about 16. She claimed, as I did, that she was in a loveless marriage and, for years, had gone to church and volunteered with church activities by herself. We both went on and on about each other without skipping a beat. I don't remember having any awkward moments.

After a while, we stopped for coffee. She didn't want to go inside, so I got our coffee while she waited in the car. When I came back with the coffee, she appeared a bit nervous. I reached over and kissed her. She kissed me back. Things became heated quickly, and we found ourselves together in a hotel room. When it was over, we both felt relieved. Her husband worked late every night at the university and rarely came home before midnight. So we ate dinner together and talked about what had just transpired. We agreed that we both had love missing in our lives and would see each other.

The relationship continued for the rest of the time while I was in Korea. I felt terrible at the end because the reason I was leaving was because I had been accepted for a job in Hawaii at pay grade GS-12; otherwise, I would have stayed in Korea until a GS-12 position was to open up at 8th Army. My leaving Korea hit Min very hard because by this time, we had fallen in love with one another, and both agreed we wanted to divorce our spouses. But by the end of February 2020, she cut all contact between us to rekindle her relationship with her husband.

But by now in the spring of 2021, Min moved back up to Seoul with her parents and decided after her youngest son was finished with high school, she would go through with a divorce. She wouldn't tell me what her husband did to her to make that final decision, but from the way she talked, it sounded like something pretty bad happened between them, and it involved the police. So when I told her I was coming back to work in Pyong-Taek, which was about an hour from her parents via train, she was ecstatic. We would both have living partners who would appreciate what each other brought to the relationship.

As I mentioned before I gave the back story, I was given notice of a tentative offer to live and work in Korea. I knew the only way to tell Ramona I wanted a divorce was to do this by Facetime, as any other way would not be kosher. I thought and prayed about it for a couple of days and decided to do it on Saturday morning after returning to my apartment from my walk. At approximately 7:00 am local time, I called Ramona on Facetime. Knowing I should not drag this out, I got right to the point. I said to her, "I am not going to be here long, so I just want to tell you I want a divorce."

Her head dropped immediately when she heard this. I had gone down this road twice but didn't follow through. She knew I was serious this time and asked, "Have you met someone?" I didn't answer since I felt it was none of her business and I was at the end of my rope with this 75/25 relationship. I ended the call and later looked online for paperwork to file for an uncontested divorce.

My daughter Mercedes wasn't happy with me and has not talked to me to this day. I don't know if she won't speak to me because I divorced her mother, I am a Trump fan, or that I put crazy posts up on Facebook for the whole world to see regarding Trump and what I knew was a stolen election. I miss her, and I wish she would respond to my messages, but alas, she wants nothing to do with me. She currently resides in Oklahoma City and works as a Probation/Parole Officer. I am so proud of what she has become, and I know it was difficult for her not to have her dad at home for all those years, but I did my best to take care of my family so we would never experience life the way we did after my retirement from the Army in 2010.

Within a month, I completed the divorce paperwork, had it notarized, and sent it to our address in Oklahoma. It was very generous, and I would leave her basically everything. Honestly, I felt such a level of betrayal from my wife that I didn't want to go back to get my things. I just wanted to move on, but I needed to make sure in doing so, she wasn't left with nothing in the wake of my decision with two pets she could not take care of.

In the proposal, I left the house valued at approximately $300,000 to her, along with a monthly payment of $1800 from my Army pension. The house was paid off from when I worked in Afghanistan, so I figured with a paid-off home and about 75 percent of my pension, this would help her out immensely. She would most likely need to get a part-time job, but the way I saw it, this offer was right for her. In the end, what I wanted was my freedom and the money I made from the US Government in Korea to be mine. She called me after she received the documents and told me that while it was a generous offer, she wanted more. My thoughts are a bit hazy on this because I couldn't believe what she was asking for, but I think she wanted me to send her something like $2500 per month, which was more than what I was receiving for a pension after taxes. She told me she would look for a mediator so we could come to a better agreement and that she would pay for it.

This particular time was very difficult for me. In addition to being alone and having to deal with everything I have described, I also had to deal with losing a person I was married to for over a quarter of a century.

The feelings I experienced were brutal; it was as if someone I loved died. I was experiencing a period of mourning in my life. I remember times when I would break down and cry. I could be sitting in my car at a stop light, or work - thank God I was alone in my office most of the time. A couple of times, I woke up in the middle of the night and just started bawling. It was the death of my marriage I was experiencing, and what made it even more difficult was the fact that my wife didn't even fight to try and save the marriage. It made me wonder if I should have filed for divorce years ago. Was she always that callous? I had told her for years that I didn't want to be alone, and she was happy as hell to be in that house by herself without me there. It took me a good while, but I got over these feelings and had no regret about filing, with one exception being that my daughter severed our relationship. I pray that she soon finds it in her heart to forgive me for whatever wrongdoing I committed.

A few months later, in the late summer, a mediator helped settle the differences. Ramona wanted me to pay $2200 per month in alimony on top of the house. She stated she was moving back to Germany to live with her mom, which I could not understand since our daughter had no family anywhere near her in Oklahoma City, but that was her choice. She said she would leave in the spring of 2022 and would need help paying the bills. I agreed to continue to give her access to the bank account after the divorce was final while she lived in the house up until she moved. I would not budge from the $1800 monthly payment, though, to which the mediator stepped in and said if this were ever to go to trial, the judge would not agree to the $2200. Our divorce was finalized in December of 2021.

Life at this time was very difficult, but the prospect of returning to a land and culture I loved helped raise my vibration. I slowly began to feel alive again, eased up quite a bit on my alcohol consumption, and adjusted my diet, cutting out meat and only eating fruits, nuts, and anything vegetables. I started listening to the Psalms while sleeping, which helped give me a good night's rest, and I started exercising more. I didn't go to the gym as often as I wanted, as mandatory vaccinations for entrance were looming, but I did get out in the open air much more than I had over the past few months. I felt closer to God right now. I know He was there with me, and I know He communicated with me through the hard times and now. I was definitely at a point where I could turn the page in my life and start the next chapter, and it felt good. It was about this time I came across my Blackhorse Brother, Minh, who immigrated to America as a baby at the end of the Vietnam War with his family and grew up in California.

Chapter 8

My Blackhorse Brother (One of Many)

Minh and I first met in 2005 when we were stationed together at the National Training Center, Fort Irwin, California, where the Army trains its organizations to prepare for war. I was the Platoon Sergeant for the Air Defense Battery 11th Armored Cavalry Regiment (Blackhorse), and Minh was my Platoon Leader. We ran into each other a few times over the years and were stationed in Korea together when I was an IG. While in Korea, we partied pretty hard together. I took him to my favorite neighborhood in Seoul, where the expats lived, and we had a great time! We had a couple of hiccups during our relationship in Korea, and I will keep those stories out of the public eye out of respect for that relationship. Whatever happened to us under the influence of alcohol was something we both learned from and put behind us. I may revisit those times at a later date, but I think in order to give a true and accurate depiction of events, it would require the collaboration of Minh and me together since perspective is everything.

At the time of my arrival, Minh worked at the Human Resources section of the USARPAC Command, known as the G1. He held the rank of Major but would soon be promoted to Lieutenant Colonel. This section was responsible for a wide range of items, to include tracking Personnel Accountability of all soldiers within the USARPAC footprint covering half of the world, regulations, assignment orders to and from USARPAC, etc. This operation required a large number of civilian and military personnel to ensure the required mission of the USARPAC Commanding General was always carried out.

Minh called me up once before the lockdown, aware of my arrival to the island since that was part of his job. We had separated from each other about a year earlier, not on good terms, but enough time passed, giving the both of us the ability to reflect on things. It was good to see Minh, and great to be back around him. He took me to his apartment on the east side of Honolulu, in Kapolei. I don't remember what floor he lived on, but his apartment was high enough that when you looked out of the window, you could see an amazing panoramic view of the beach and the Pacific Ocean. Looking out at the sunrise in the morning was absolutely majestic. I felt this was a peaceful bliss Minh needed since the job he worked was highly stressful in a Four Star Command covering half of the globe.

The apartment complex he lived in was interesting because it was a one-stop shop. You didn't need a car to go out for entertainment because almost everything you needed was around you. If you wanted to drink, eat, go to the movies, or go grocery shopping, everything was close by because it was all a part of the same complex. I remember leaving his apartment to get on the elevator that took us to the bar. I don't vividly remember everything about the bar, since I had only been there once, but I remember we stopped in there for a couple of beers before we left and went to the Dave & Buster's restaurant around the corner.

We ordered burgers and wings to go along with our beers, and I brought him up to speed on everything in Korea after he departed. We talked a little bit about what happened between the two of us, and then we moved on from the distant memory. I told Minh about Min and thought it ironic that I had two Min(h)'s in my life. I opened my soul to him about her and how she made me feel alive after almost a decade of loneliness. And he knew and could feel exactly what I was talking about. Minh and I shared very similar lives. We were both military men who were geographically separated from our families, and both of us knew what it was like to be lonely while providing financial support to our families while we were away. That was sort of a bond that connected the two of us. You see, it is common for those current and former military members to be geographically separated from their families (in my case, because I was an overseas contractor), but what is not common is the fact that only a few live separately for years at a time, only reuniting with families once or twice a year for short periods.

In my case, there were a few times during the last decade when I didn't see my family for 15-18 months. This was due to the volatility of the contractor job market. I remember during the contractor drawdown in Afghanistan when DynCorp International laid people off while they were home on leave after the military decided what cuts to make. Most of us stayed over there to avoid this from happening. Getting back to Minh, he had been separated from his family probably longer than I was. So we both knew how difficult things could get and realized how we could lean on one another. We went to a few bars afterward, not to get hammered, but so Minh could show me the places he frequented when he wasn't at work. I had a great time and stayed in the spare room of his place. This was the last time I saw Minh before the pandemic. Due to whatever circumstances I cannot say, we didn't hang out together once the lockdowns were in place.

Fast forward to the spring of 2021, when Minh called me out of the blue, he wanted to set up a meeting to talk about business. "Business?" I thought. "I wonder what type of business Minh wanted to talk to me about." He had my curiosity, and it had been a long minute since we had seen each other, so I looked forward to getting together. We met at the Post Exchange on Fort Shafter, the military installation where we both worked. Fort Shafter had a small exchange store; it was more like a shoppette. For those unaware of what a shoppette is, picture something like a Sheetz or 7-11 gas station, with a small area of tables to sit down and eat.

Anyway, we met there for lunch and ordered sandwiches from Subway, getting a six-inch club sandwich with a meal. Minh ordered chips, and I liked my cookies, so I asked for the M&M chocolate chip cookies to go with my sandwich. I think the dining area only consisted of five or six tables with two chair settings, and they all had big plastic plexiglass dividers right smack in the middle of these small tables.

This was the first time since the lockdowns began a year earlier that I had been inside eating with a guest. I remember sitting down eating here and other military eateries on Oahu, but always by myself. This was the first time I sat at one of these and held any type of conversation with anybody but myself. I laugh while I say that, because I would constantly talk to myself, because who else did I have to talk to? Joking aside, I just don't have that ability to think thoughts inside my head. I need to play them out, hence the reason I talk to myself. Well, I might just be a little crazy as well (insert laughter here).

So we ate and conversed at the same time. It was really good to see Minh, after not seeing him in more than a year while stationed there together. We talked about the pandemic and how it affected us both (I brought up the plexiglass earlier because I remember getting frustrated at not being able to hear everything Minh was talking about. What a nuisance they were, as they obstructed the conversation and made it so unappealing to sit and have a personal conversation, but we pushed on). I have no idea why I hadn't contacted him before he reached out. It probably would have helped me cope with everything better. However, I have learned that God is involved in all matters, whether we know it or not. And through this journey of fire and brimstone, I have learned much.

After all of the pleasantries and catching up from the last time we spent time together in the beginning, Minh was ready to get down to business. He mentioned his office was going to add an operations position, and I was the first person he thought of to fill it. He said whoever would fill the position would coordinate with military units all around the Pacific Rim to set up training and fill the necessary positions in war gaming scenarios. This would require much research on the part of the candidate regarding the different weapon system capabilities. My time in the OPFOR (Opposing Force) at Fort Irwin and my level of expertise through research in my IG duties most likely made me a right fit for this job, along with the fact Minh had known me for years and understood completely my strengths and weaknesses.

This position would require a lot of travel, as military exercises are conducted all the time, mostly by computer these days, but augmented by 'boots on the ground' as well. I was interested and knew I would excel at this position because I have a remarkable ability to go along and get along, and my work ethic is second to none. As he talked about this, I knew I would have an issue. I immediately told Minh that I would love the position. However, rumors were swirling everywhere there would come a time when the COVID-19 vaccination shots would become mandatory. He acknowledged my concern and we both agreed that was a bridge to cross at a later date.

As a friend, I couldn't let the conversation go without telling him that I had received a tentative offer to go back to Korea and work in the same IG office I'd worked in as my last assignment in a military uniform. I mentioned that at this time, the job offer is only tentative, and until I knew I passed my overseas physical, I didn't consider myself fully having the job. He nodded in acknowledgment and congratulated me but said I should still apply for the job in case things didn't work out with the position in Korea. So that's exactly what I did. We made plans to hang out over the weekend at the end of our lunch.

Within a couple of weeks of our meeting, I received word from Korea that I fulfilled all requirements of the onboarding process, passed my overseas physical, and received the expected arrival date. There would be a change to the date of arrival because arriving too early would make me ineligible for a government housing stipend that I just wouldn't be able to afford payment on. My arrival date would ultimately change from sometime in July to the end of November, to reset the two-year clock that a Department of the Army Civilian had to be away from an overseas assignment before the return.

After receiving word of my pending assignment, I contacted Minh and made plans to go out that weekend. I told him that I had received word from Korea that everything had been finalized and that I would go in that direction. He admitted that if he were in my position, he too would choose to go to Korea because we both loved it so much there. Still, he admitted disappointment because he wanted to work with me again, but I asked him if he had someone else in mind who he thought could do a terrific job. He said there was a recently retired Sergeant First Class (Pay Grade level E-7) who needed a job. He was very capable and excelled at his duties. I explained that I felt it was my place to go to Korea instead of staying in Hawaii and that because of that, he could find work easily after leaving the Army. I had discussed my difficulties in finding employment after retirement with Minh a few times in the past. So, we both knew this would be a blessing for this young man. It turned out later he was the perfect fit.

Minh and I would stay in touch after this, and we would hang out during some weekends. It wasn't too often because his job had him working late nights and traveling quite a bit, but when he could fit me into his schedule, we would often hang together during the weekend. Some weekends, we drank a little heavier than others, but at no time did we get crazy with the amount of consumption that we had in Korea. Drinking in Korea was at a whole other level, but I'll have to tell that story another time.

In the end, I would consider Minh in my top three. We haven't spoken for a while, although my other Blackhorse Brother, Rob, met up with him during a conference he traveled to, and they called me by video from a bar as I was getting ready for work in Pennsylvania around 4:00 am in May of 2023. Rob comes into the story later, as I stayed at his (his mom's) house for a year. Around the time I departed Hawaii, Minh came through in a very big way for me, but we aren't at that part of the story yet, so let's move on and come back to that when the time comes.

Chapter 9

Uncertain Times Ahead

By now, it was the summer of 2021. Things seemed to be getting better for me. Though Hawaii still wasn't fully back to being one hundred percent pre-Covid normal, many of the restrictions had now been lifted. We could go out to restaurants, although I really disliked having to wear a mask inside, walking to my table with it around my face, and then taking it off when sitting down at the table. Those who remember the television show *Get Smart* and remember the "Cone of Silence" can appreciate how I felt about the "Cone of Protection" around each restaurant table. This was some amazing technology that stopped Covid in its tracks! As long as you were sitting at your table, Covid could not come to take you away! But the minute you get up to use the bathroom, you'd better have that mask on - make sure it is over your nose - otherwise the 'vid' is gonna get you.

The whole thing was so ridiculous, yet many were lulled to sleep somehow, and they fell for this garbage. Many bars and restaurants closed early, too, as if the Covid boogeyman would come outside after a certain hour if you weren't inside your home with the blood of a lamb placed atop your door so it passed you by. Honestly, the mind-control programming of COVID-19, and the following 24/7 propaganda on television with the dancing commercials and late-night comedy sketches such as Colbert's dancing Covid shots became highly effective propaganda that scared the living daylights out of many unsuspecting Americans and people living throughout the world. Thank God some of us were not buying what they were selling, and we continued to speak out against it whenever and however we could. The digital battlefield is where I spoke out the loudest.

Min and I had quite a few conversations about my return to Korea. She insisted there was no turning back for her regarding her marriage. I didn't ask her what exactly happened, but by her earlier correspondence with me, I think whatever it was must have been pretty dramatic. I figured she would tell me when she felt comfortable telling me about her experience. Her youngest son would finish high school the following year, and he stayed with his father in Daegu while Min stayed with her parents in Seoul. She would begin filing paperwork for divorce proceedings around the time of my departure from Hawaii. I was looking forward to seeing her again and missed her dearly.

The change was difficult for her, moving back with her parents after so many years away. She looked for work and found it in the school system, where she taught children athletics and dance. She had been a ballet dancer in her earlier years and took me to my first and only ballet experience in Daegu not long before I departed Korea in 2019. She incorporated her ballet dancing techniques into her Pilates, and I was lucky to experience that in her studio. She was just an all-around interesting child of God, scarred from life as I was, and we completed the emptiness inside one another. It wasn't long before Min found a place of worship in Seoul, and she volunteered her services regularly at the church. There would be more difficult times ahead, and she would need His guidance and refuge.

Other great news came out of Korea on the job front. It was now July 2021, and all of the offices on Fort Shafter had returned to work full-time after 15 months of telework. My old boss was the Deputy IG for the 19th Expeditionary Sustainment Command (ESC) in Daegu. I talked with him on the phone one day when he told me he had applied for the Deputy IG position at 8th Army, the office I was headed to. Now, his position was a GS-13 position, which provided a considerable salary increase from the position I held at GS-12. If he were to be hired at 8th Army to the GS-14 position, I could apply for his position. I had already been at the

GS-12 level for almost two years and only needed to be at the current level for one year before being eligible for the next level position.

Typically, with overseas assignments, the government saves money from having to move people from the US if there are eligible people already in-country. This was the case with my old boss, Rob. He was one of the more knowledgeable IGs I knew of and was honest. I learned a few things from him, and though we had a rocky beginning together, we respected each other, and in the end, I considered him a friend. By the time I arrived in November, the chance was good that he would be moved and I could apply to his old position, knowing the likelihood of taking over as deputy would be high.

By late July, I received my FINAL offer letter for Korea. I knew and accepted verbally, but this would make things official. I was stoked at receiving the email in my inbox. I told everybody about it - my co-workers, friends, friends on social media, etc. I remember calling my close friends Luanna and Nav in Seoul over video and letting them know my official arrival date. We hadn't talked, so we caught up on everything. I told them that I had finally decided to pull the plug on my marriage and let them know I had to accomplish a couple of things before finalizing, including speaking with the mediator and Ramona.

Nav knew my stance on the vaccine, and he asked me what I was going to do if, by the time I was to report, the vaccine was mandated for federal employees. I told Nav that due to what I had known about the vaccines and the censored reports I witnessed showing how dangerous the vaccine was, there was no way I would stay on with the federal workforce if that be the case. I assured him, however, that I wasn't going to let that stress me and I would just cross that bridge when I came to it.

I loved my relationship with Luanna and Nav. Politically, we were on opposite sides of the fence, but our love for each other was unconditional, and I don't believe we would let politics stand in the way of our relationship. I still feel that way to this day. In the end, it was probably my fault as to why we lost touch. I was back home in St. Louis and had just left a job I was in over my head with when I recorded a birthday message Luanna requested some of their friends to do. I was drunk when I did it, and it wasn't that I said anything bad; after all, I'm a happy drunk. I think the issue was I probably looked pretty pathetic doing it. It was one of the lowest points in my life, at that time anyway. I haven't reached out since, especially with where the lines are drawn in this Covid PSYOP with my sometimes crazy posts on social media.

Anyway, during the summer of 2021, we were very much in contact, and I needed to let them know. I have attached my FINAL offer letter to 8th Army Inspector General Office to give perspective because I unexpectedly received a revised offer letter almost five months later that would turn my life upside down. Both offers are listed below. I list only the subject and body of the revised offer letter after the original below. Notice in the original letter it never stated that the US Government reserved the right to adjust any requirements in order to qualify for the position.

* * *

From: <usastaffingoffice@opm.gov>

Date: Thu, Jul 22, 2021 at 21:59

Subject: Official Offer Letter for Inspector General, GS-1801-12

To: <moneil5150@xxxxxx.com>

CC: <XXXXXXX.M.KIM7.CIV@mail.mil>, <dale.l.XXXXXX62.civ@mail.mil>, <xxxxx.hong@us.army.mil>

Dear Michael O'Neil,

Congratulations! This letter serves as your final job offer and acceptance as an Inspector General, GS-1801-12 step 02 with the U.S. Army, Pacific in PYONG TAEK, No States Available. You will receive a salary of $69,057 Per Year. This does not include Post Allowance or Living Quarters Allowance; these will be calculated separately.

Dale XXXXXX will be contacting you shortly with all orientation procedures and next steps.

This is a permanent position.

This position requires the following Conditions of

Employment. If you are unable to obtain/maintain these requirements, you may be separated from the position and Federal employment. By accepting this job offer, you are acknowledging and agreeing to these Conditions of Employment.

1. Incumbent must be willing to attend and successfully complete the Department of the Army Inspector General Course either as initial or refresher training and the Department of Defense Joint IG Course.

2. Position has been designated Emergency Essential (EE) in support of mobilization and wartime mission. If designated E-E, employee will be required to remain in the overseas position in the event of hostilities or mobilization until relieved by proper authority. E-E employees are required to undergo nuclear-biological and chemical training and to participate in readiness tests, mobilization, alerts, and field training exercises. Employee must pass a medical examination and receive required immunizations for the overseas/deployed location. Prior to appointment to the position, employee will sign a statement agreeing to the E-E condition of employment.

3. Applicants must obtain and maintain a SECRET security clearance.

Note: 1. Temporary Duty away from duty location is up to 25% of the time.

The Department of Army is committed to the highest ethical standards and as an employee, you will be covered by the criminal conflict of interest statutes and the Standards of Ethical Conduct for Employees of the Executive Branch. You will be required to complete new employee ethics training within 3 months of your appointment.

Please be advised that as a supervisor or if you become a supervisor, you are also subject to 5 Code of Federal Regulations (C.F.R.) § 2638.103, Government Ethics Responsibilities of Supervisors:

Every supervisor in the executive branch has a heightened personal responsibility for advancing government ethics. It is imperative that supervisors serve as models of ethical behavior for subordinates. Supervisors have a responsibility to help ensure that subordinates are aware of their ethical obligations under the Standards of Conduct and that subordinates know how to contact agency ethics officials. Supervisors are also responsible for working with agency ethics officials to help resolve conflicts of interest and enforce government ethics laws and regulations, including those requiring certain employees to file financial disclosure reports. In addition, supervisors are responsible, when requested, for assisting agency ethics officials in evaluating potential conflicts of interest and identifying positions subject to financial disclosure requirements. You are required to review the "14 General Principles of Ethical Conduct", located at : https://www.oge.gov/Web/OGE.nsf/Resources/14+General+Princi ples+Card. You may contact the Ethics Office for additional information on applicable ethics requirements.

We look forward to your arrival on 11/21/2021 and welcome you to the U.S. Army, Pacific, HHB.

To record your response to this official offer and access the entrance on duty system, visit: https://onboard.usastaffing.gov/?newhire=HOXJG-OBEG&type=official

If you have any questions regarding your new position, please contact me at chris.xxxxx.civ@mail.mil, caitlin.m.xxxxxxxx.civ@mail.mil or 315XXXXX, 315-757-XXXX.

Respectfully,

Chris XXXXX, Caitlin XXXXXXX

* * *

From: usastaffingoffice@opm.gov (on behalf of CATHY xxxxx)

Sent: 11/4/2021 0:59 EDT

Subject: AMENDED Official Offer for Inspector General, GS-1801-12, PYONG TAEK, No States Available (COVID-19 Vaccination Requirement)

Michael O'Neil,

This is an amendment to the official job offer of employment you received for Inspector General, GS-1801-12 with U.S. Army, Pacific. In addition to the requirements initially stated in your official job offer, it will be contingent on you providing appropriate documentation of proof of COVID-19 vaccination by Monday, November 22, 2021.

You will be receiving a separate notification with the contact information of the Hiring Manager who will provide the process for submitting proof of vaccination and/or requesting an exemption. Documentation of proof of COVID-19 vaccination must be received by the Hiring Manager by Monday, November 22, 2021.

You can provide a copy of the record of immunization from a health care provider or pharmacy, a copy of the COVID-19 Vaccination Record Card, a copy of medical records documenting the vaccination, a copy of immunization records from a public health or state immunization information system, or a copy of any other official documentation containing required data points (type of vaccine administered, date(s) of administration, and the name of the health care professional(s) or clinic site(s) administering the vaccine(s)).

Follow the instructions in the separate notification; proof of vaccination should NOT be submitted using the USA Staffing entrance on duty system OR to your HR contact.

To respond to this amended official job offer, please reply via email to Cathy N. xxxxx at cathy.n.xxxxx.-civ@army.mil by Monday, November 8, 2021.

Respectfully,

Cathy N. xxxxx

* * *

I address this now because, in addition to everything that has transpired over the past four years with Covid, the election, and the ensuing censorship and propaganda around all of it, the looming federal vaccine mandates on federal employees, military, and many other organizations turned my life upside down. I knew, however, that it was necessary to stand my ground, no matter what horrors I would face with my non-compliance. God would be with me every step of the way, and I needed Him because I could see no other way to survive the coming onslaught without His protection.

It was about this time I stumbled upon what Senator Ron Johnson was attempting to bring awareness regarding the dangers of the COVID-19 vaccines and the letters he wrote to the various health agencies, which mostly went unanswered. Like other Patriots in the Truth Movement, Senator Johnson shed light on the Covid vaccines. Senator Johnson sent letters to directors of the Center for Disease Control & Prevention (CDC), Food and Drug Administration (FDA), Dr. Fauci, and others. Senator Johnson was a beacon of light for those of us who knew something was just not right. Of course, he was censored by the "fact checkers" and that joke of a site called Snopes, but he persisted with almost a dozen letters, many of which were not addressed by those such as Rochelle Walensky (CDC), Janet Woodcock (FDA), Albert Bourla (Pfizer), or Dr. Fauci. A few examples of Sen. Johnson's correspondence to these agencies are listed in the picture section. More information regarding

Sen. Johnson's dogged pursuit of the truth about COVID-19 and vaccines can be found on his official government website.

Even though my life seemed to be taking a turn in a positive direction with my near future move back to Korea, I couldn't help but feel the noose beginning to tighten because of talk about federal mandates of the Covid vaccination. The Sergeant Major in my office and I were the last two holdouts. We served together in 2005 at Fort Irwin in the 11th Armored Cavalry Regiment, but I had not known him then. I felt aghast when I saw him at Trippler Army Medical Center while taking my physical when he told me he was getting the shot. I had gained much respect for his stand against taking it, and by this time, I felt my heart in my throat. If he was taking the shot, I knew it was only a matter of time before it would be forced upon the rest of us.

I kept moving forward, though, and I had many conversations with Dan in his office, not only about Covid, but about a lot of things pertaining to the past year. Every time I found new information I learned about Covid, I would present it to him, and he listened. He told me a story of how, in a staff meeting, the USARPAC surgeon said those with Covid were getting Myocarditis. I told Dan the information the surgeon was putting out was incorrect. I talked about the numerous videos and podcasts I had seen with those such as Drs. Robert Malone, Sherry Tenpenney, Paul Alexander, Peter McCullough, Carrie Medej and many others, who stated they had not seen so many cases of Myocarditis until after the administration of these vaccines. These people were, and still are, on the frontlines of this war, even though they have been discredited and called purveyors of disinformation by those in the media and Big Tech.

My military first-line supervisor, whose name I will not reveal here, constantly asked me if I was going to get the vaccine. I told him that I wasn't and cited the Nuremberg Code. He shrugged it off and said that the vaccine would eventually be mandatory, and if so, I would need to look for a different job. This man was interesting. He was very bright but lacked wisdom, maturity, and empathy. I actually liked him for a while and, at times, would give him recommendations based on life experience. However, I could see a change in his perception of me when I wouldn't follow with the rest. There was a day early on in August when we conducted a conference call with my future office in Korea regarding a topic within the Assistance & Investigations (A&I) Division. My supervisor began with introductions (we all knew each other), and when he came to my introduction, he said, "And Mike O'Neil is here, who you may or may not be working with in the near future." I heard this and was outraged. He had no business saying this at all. This would be my future assignment, and this guy is putting my business out there on the street. We had already begun having somewhat of a strained relationship, and I should have said something to him then, but I decided it best to keep my mouth shut. I don't remember if I told Dan about this, but I know I did not keep it inside, as I was furious with this statement.

On the divorce front, the mediator contacted me for a time to have a three-way talk. I agreed, and shortly after, we had our meeting. The meeting was supposed to be video, but since she was having technical problems, we conducted it via teleconference. Ramona started first and immediately talked about the money. It wasn't as high as $2,500 but more than $1,800. She also explained her plans to move to Germany. This is when I agreed I would give her full access to the money after the divorce until the time she left. I agreed to everything she wanted, including the dog and cat, which was pretty much a no-brainer since they already lived with her, but I would not budge on the amount. As of December 15, 2021, Ramona would become my ex-wife after more than 27 years of marriage. I would never look back.

The Department of Defense released Supplement 23, covering Force Protection Guidance, on September 7, 2021. This document established weekly testing procedures for all federal employees and contractors and outlined how these procedures were followed. To enter any federal building on a US Government military installation, one would be required to show their testing status or be refused entry. All members were required to fill out a form titled DD Form 3150 *Certificate of Vaccination* and present the form upon request when entering any federal building as well. I was not ever requested to present either in my short time left working with the government, but the fact this was being requested was unprecedented and downright scary when you think about it.

Regarding the testing, it was a bit more lenient, so I got creative. We were allowed home tests, so I bought a couple of tests from the CVS drugstore. I always felt the Covid tests were a bunch of BS. I mean, why is it required to swab the inside of your mouth before jamming a long stem cotton swab up your nose and reaching your brain? Who in the world came up with this? You could just as easily spit on the swab and test the saliva for the presence of Covid. And that's exactly what I did. Since I wasn't required to stand in front of someone while taking the test, I didn't have to shove that cotton swab all the way to my brain, breaching my blood-brain barrier in the process. Thank God I never had that done. I know many millions were subjected to that nonsense, and I wanted no part of it. To the credit of my chain of command, they never asked me to show them my test. I only showed it to the CIG and the Deputy IG when the Command IG asked me to explain how I go through the weekly testing process. I carried the same test in my pocket for the duration of my time there.

On September 9th, the President signed Executive Order 14043 mandating federal employees to take the COVID-19 vaccine. On October 1, 2021, EO 14043 was followed up with a DOD Memorandum that gave guidance on deadlines for when vaccination was to be completed. The timeline coincided with my arrival in Korea, as the memorandum outlined the second dose must be administered no later than November 8th, and I was scheduled to report by November 21st. By now, I began to feel the pressure, and the only thing I could do was let this whole scenario play out. These were not fun times to be living and working within this environment, and I endured a few sleepless nights because of it. The clock was ticking, and my future was uncertain and in the balance. What lay ahead was frightening!

United States Senate

WASHINGTON, DC 20510

August 26, 2021

Janet Woodcock, M.D.
Acting Commissioner
Food and Drug Administration
10903 New Hampshire Ave.
Silver Spring, MD 20993

Dear Acting Commissioner Woodcock:

On August 23, 2021, the FDA reissued the Emergency Use Authorization (EUA) for the Pfizer-BioNTech COVID-19 vaccine.[1] This vaccine is currently available and used in the United States. At the same time, the FDA announced its approval of the biologics license application submitted by BioNTech Manufacturing GmbH for Comirnaty (COVID-19 Vaccine, mRNA) against COVID-19 for individuals 16 years of age and older.[2] According to the FDA, "there is not sufficient approved vaccine [Comirnaty] available for distribution" in the U.S.[3]

In the letter that reissued the EUA for the Pfizer-BioNTech COVID-19 vaccine, the FDA stated that Comirnaty and the Pfizer-BioNTech COVID-19 vaccines are "legally distinct with certain differences that do not impact safety or effectiveness."[4] That statement, together with the fact that the FDA issued two distinct letters – one extending the EUA for the vaccine used in the U.S. and the other granting the FDA approval of the Comirnaty vaccine used in Europe and other countries – has caused a great deal of confusion.

As I stated to you in my letter dated August 22, 2021, "I see no need to rush the FDA approval process for any of the three COVID-19 vaccines. Expediting the process appears to only serve the political purpose of imposing and enforcing vaccine mandates."[5] Because the FDA-approved Comirnaty vaccine is not generally available in the U.S., but the Pfizer-BioNTech COVID-19 vaccine will continue to be used in the U.S. under a reissued EUA, the FDA seems to be confirming my suspicion.

---

[1] Letter to Elisa Harkins, Pfizer Inc., from Denise Hinton, Chief Scientist, U.S. Food and Drug Administration, Aug. 23, 2021 available at https://www.fda.gov/media/150386/download.
[2] Letter to Amit Patel, BioNTech Manufacturing GmbH, from Mary Malarkey, Director, Office of Compliance and Biologics Quality, U.S. Food and Drug Administration, and Marion Gruber, Director, Office of Vaccines Research and Review, U.S. Food and Drug Administration, Aug. 23, 2021 available at https://www.fda.gov/media/151710/download.
[3] Letter to Elisa Harkins, Pfizer Inc., from Denise Hinton, Chief Scientist, U.S. Food and Drug Administration at 5, Aug. 23, 2021 available at https://www.fda.gov/media/150386/download (See footnote 9).
[4] *Id.* at 2 (See footnote 8).
[5] Letter from Ron Johnson, U.S. Senator, to Janet Woodcock, Acting Commissioner, U.S. Food and Drug Administration, et al., Aug. 22, 2021.

Acting Commissioner Janet Woodcock
Aug. 26, 2021
Page 2

In order to address the confusion created by the FDA's August 23, 2021 letters, I am asking that you expeditiously provide answers to the following questions:

1) Why didn't the FDA grant full licensure for the Pfizer-BioNTech vaccine that is in use and available in the U.S.?

2) How are the Comirnaty and Pfizer-BioNTech COVID-19 vaccines "legally distinct" and what are the "certain differences"?

3) There is no doubt that the FDA's action will lead to more vaccine mandates and increased pressure on those currently choosing not to get vaccinated. Your letter to Pfizer suggests that "there is not sufficient approved vaccine available for distribution."[6] Is there sufficient supply in the U.S. of the Comirnaty vaccine to ensure that those being vaccinated under mandates will be receiving the FDA-approved version? Or is it more likely (or certain) that they will be vaccinated using the vaccine administered under the reissued EUA?

4) If there is insufficient supply of Comirnaty vaccines for those succumbing to the coercion of mandates, isn't the FDA *de facto* endorsing vaccine mandates utilizing EUA vaccines?

5) Will individuals who receive either vaccine be afforded the same legal protections if they are injured by the vaccine? If not, why not?

I look forward to receiving a response to this limited number of questions no later than August 30, 2021. Your answers are crucial to Americans who will now be forced into making potentially life-altering decisions in response to the employer, military and educational mandates that your August 23, 2021 letters have triggered. I will also be sending you a more detailed follow-up letter to your inadequate response to my August 22, 2021 letter in the next few days.

Sincerely,

Ron Johnson

Ron Johnson
U.S. Senator

[6] Letter to Elisa Harkins, Pfizer Inc., from Denise Hinton, Chief Scientist, U.S. Food and Drug Administration at 5, Aug. 23, 2021 available at https://www.fda.gov/media/150386/download (See footnote 9).

United States Senate

WASHINGTON, DC 20510

September 7, 2021

Janet Woodcock, M.D.
Acting Commissioner
Food and Drug Administration
10903 New Hampshire Ave.
Silver Spring MD 20993

Peter Marks, M.D., PhD.
Director
Center for Biologics Evaluation and Research
Food and Drug Administration
10903 New Hampshire Ave.
Silver Spring MD 20993

Dear Drs. Woodcock and Marks:

On July 20, 2021, European researchers released a preprint study that examined the connection between the SARS-CoV-2 spike protein (S-protein) and potential damage to heart and other organ tissue.[1] This study indicates the S-protein, which is also produced by the mRNA COVID-19 vaccines, including the U.S. Food and Drug Administration (FDA) approved Corminaty vaccine, may be attaching to and damaging heart and other organ tissue. Given the technology used in the mRNA vaccines, I am concerned that the same S-protein-related damages to human tissue caused by the SARS-CoV-2 virus could also manifest itself in recipients of the mRNA vaccines. The title, lead author, publication information, abstract, and clinical perspective are provided below:

> **The SARS-CoV-2 Spike protein disrupts human cardiac pericytes function through CD147-receptor-mediated signalling: a potential non-infective mechanism of COVID-19 microvascular disease**
> By: Elisa Avolio, PhD1, et al.
>
> bioRxiv preprint doi: https://doi.org/10.1101/2020.12.21.423721; this version posted July 20, 2021. The copyright holder for this preprint (which was not certified by peer review) is the author/funder.
>
> **ABSTRACT**
>
> Severe coronavirus disease 2019 (COVID-19) manifests as a life-threatening microvascular syndrome. The severe acute respiratory syndrome coronavirus 2

[1] Elisa Avolio, et al, The SAS-CoV-2 Spike protein disrupts human cardiac pericytes function through CD147-receptor-mediated signalling: a potential non-infective mechanism of COVID-19 microvascular disease, BioRxiv (preprint) July 20 2021, available at https://www.biorxiv.org/content/10.1101/2020.12.21.423721v2.full.pdf

(SARS-CoV-2) uses the Spike (S) protein to engage with its receptors and infect host cells. To date, it is still not known whether heart vascular pericytes (PCs) are infected by SARS-CoV-2, and if the S protein alone provokes PC dysfunction. Here, we aimed to investigate the effects of the S protein on primary human cardiac PC signaling and function. Results show, for the first time, that cardiac PCs are not permissive to SARS-CoV-2 infection in vitro, whilst a recombinant S protein alone elicits functional alterations in PCs. This was documented as: (1) increased migration, (2) reduced ability to support endothelial cell (EC) network formation on Matrigel, (3) secretion of pro-inflammatory molecules typically involved in the cytokine storm, and (4) production of pro-apoptotic factors responsible for EC death. Next, adopting a blocking strategy against the S protein receptors angiotensin-converting enzyme 2 (ACE2) and CD147, we discovered that the S protein stimulates the phosphorylation/activation of the extracellular signal-regulated kinase 1/2 (ERK1/2) through the CD147 receptor, but not ACE2, in PCs. The neutralisation of CD147, either using a blocking antibody or mRNA silencing, reduced ERK1/2 activation and rescued PC function in the presence of the S protein. In conclusion, *our findings suggest that circulating S protein prompts vascular PC dysfunction, potentially contributing to establishing microvascular injury in organs distant from the site of infection.* This mechanism may have clinical and therapeutic implications.

Clinical perspective

- Severe COVID-19 manifests as a microvascular syndrome, but whether SARS-CoV-2 infects and damages heart vascular pericytes (PCs) remains unknown.

- We provide evidence that cardiac PCs are not infected by SARS-CoV-2. Importantly, we show that the recombinant S protein alone elicits cellular signalling through the CD147 receptor in cardiac PCs, thereby inducing cell dysfunction and microvascular disruption in vitro.

- *This study suggests that soluble S protein can potentially propagate damage to organs distant from sites of infection, promoting microvascular injury.* Blocking the CD147 receptor in patients may help protect the vasculature not only from infection, but also from the collateral damage caused by the S protein.[2]

As you are well aware, I have been concerned about safety signals emanating from Centers for Disease Control and Prevention/FDA's Vaccine Adverse Event Reporting System (VAERS) since April of this year, when I first raised the issue with Dr. Francis Collins in a meeting with other Republican Senators.[3] I have been disappointed that federal health agencies seem to have ignored or dismissed the data reported from their own early warning system.

[2] *Id.* at 1-2 (emphasis added).
[3] Meeting with Francis Collins, Director, National Institutes of Health, and Republican Senators, Apr. 27, 2021.

Drs. Woodcock and Marks
September 7, 2021
Page 3

As of August 27, 2021, VAERS is reporting 13,911 deaths and 650,077 total adverse events worldwide following receipt of a COVID-19 vaccine.[4] Of the 13,911 deaths, 4,909 (35.3%) have occurred on Day 0, 1, or 2 following vaccination. I fully understand that VAERS does not prove causation, but 35.3% of deaths occurring so soon after vaccination should cause serious concern. Furthermore, VAERS is known to significantly underreport adverse events, raising concerns that the 13,911 deaths and 650,077 adverse events does not provide the full picture. To give perspective, since VAERS's inception, there have been a total of 1,838 deaths reports for flu vaccines over a period of 31 years, or an average of 59 vaccine death reports per year.

Unfortunately, many in the medical profession and most in the mainstream and social media have followed federal health agencies' lead and ignored or dismissed vaccine safety concerns and the growing number of vaccine injuries. This, combined with the agencies' dismissive attitude toward natural immunity, is creating dangerous societal fault lines and strife regarding vaccine mandates and passports.

Over the weekend, a number of medical doctors and researchers contacted me concerning the significance of this July 20 preprint study describing the dangerous mechanism of action of the S-protein. The purpose of this letter is to make sure you are aware of the study and request a response regarding your interpretation of it. In addition, as I have yet to receive a response to my August 26, 2021 letter, I ask that you provide an immediate response regarding the confusion FDA created over its approval of Pfizer's Comirnaty vaccine.[5]

Sincerely,

Ron Johnson
U.S. Senator

---

[4] United States Department of Health and Human Services (DHHS), Public Health Service (PHS), Centers for Disease Control (CDC) / Food and Drug Administration (FDA), Vaccine Adverse Event Reporting System (VAERS) 1990 - 08/27/2021, CDC WONDER On-line Database. Accessed at http://wonder.cdc.gov/vaers.html on Sep 7, 2021 11:39:21 AM.

[5] Letter to Janet Woodcock, M.D., Acting Commissioner, U.S. Food and Drug Administration, from Ron Johnson, U.S. Senator, Aug. 26, 2021.

United States Senate

WASHINGTON, DC 20510

September 15, 2021

Anthony S. Fauci, M.D.
Director
National Institute of Allergy and Infectious Diseases
5601 Fishers Lane
Bethesda, MD 20892

Rochelle P. Walensky, M.D., MPH
Director
Centers for Disease Control and Prevention
1600 Clifton Road
Atlanta, GA 30329

Janet Woodcock, M.D.
Acting Commissioner
Food and Drug Administration
10903 New Hampshire Ave
Silver Spring, MD 20993

Dear Drs. Fauci, Walensky, and Woodcock:

On September 9, 2021, President Biden announced vaccine mandates in both the public and private sectors without making any exceptions for those who have been previously infected with COVID-19 and have natural immunity.[1] When asked to comment on the effectiveness of natural immunity against the virus based on recent studies from Israel, Dr. Anthony Fauci stated he did not "have a real firm answer" on that.[2] Almost 20 months into the pandemic, it is shocking that the chief medical advisor to the president does not have a firm grasp on the effectiveness of natural immunity, but still promotes freedom-robbing vaccine mandates. This administration clearly does not want the public to question whether natural immunity is more effective than vaccines. As President Biden revealingly declared, the vaccine mandate "is not about freedom or

---

[1] Speech by President Joseph R. Biden on COVID-19, Sept. 9, 2021, transcript available at https://www.nytimes.com/2021/09/09/us/politics/biden-vaccine-mandates-transcript.html.

[2] See Yair Golderg, et al, Protection of previous SARS CoV-2 infection is similar to that of BNT162b22 vaccine protection: A three-month nationwide experience from Israel, Apr. 24, 2021, (preprint) available at https://www.medrxiv.org/content/10.1101/2021.04.20.21255670v1, Sivan Gazit, et al, Comparing SARS-CoV-2 natural immunity to vaccine-induced immunity: reinfections versus breakthrough infections, Aug. 25, 2021, (preprint) available at https://www.medrxiv.org/content/10.1101/2021.08.24.21262415v1; Anderson Cooper 360, CNN, Sept. 9, 2021, available at https://podcasts.google.com/feed/aHR0cHM6Ly93d3cub21ueWNvbnRlbnQuY29tL2QvcGxheWxpc3QvZDgzZjUyZTQtMjQ1NS00N2Y0LTk4MmUtYWI3OTAxMjBiOTU0L2E2YzU3ZjAxLWQyOWYtNDU1Ni1iZTRiLWFiODYwMDJmNWJjNS9mM2JiZDY1OC01ZWRmLTQ3OWEtOWFhNy1hYjg2MDAyZjViZDcvcG9kY2FzdC5yc3M/episode/NDEwOWExM2QtMzAxNS00OWYxLWI2OGQtYWQ5ZjAwMDYyMzBk?hl=en&ved=2ahUKEwi8r7auhfXyAhXbKFkFHXrfCB0QieUEegQIAhAF&ep=6 (time stamp at 11:44).

September 15, 2021
Page 2

personal choice."[3] This administration's decision to disregard the effectiveness of natural immunity and demand vaccination ignores current data and is an assault on all Americans' civil liberties.

The Centers for Disease Control and Prevention (CDC) and the Food and Drug Administration (FDA) have openly admitted that they have not fully studied natural immunity, while also promoting vaccination over natural immunity. The CDC recommends that, regardless of prior infection status, individuals should be vaccinated as "experts do not yet know how long you are protected from getting sick again after recovering from COVID-19."[4] The FDA has also stated "[a]t this time, researchers do not know whether the presence of antibodies means that you are immune to COVID-19; or if you are immune, how long it will last."[5]

Recent studies in Israel, however, appear to show that natural immunity may provide similar or even better protection than vaccines in the fight against COVID-19. In one preprint study, researchers found that, in terms of protecting against COVID-19, previous SARS-CoV-2 infection provided similar protection compared to the BioNTech vaccine.[6] Another preprint study from Israel found that individuals with previous infection had 13 times the protection from the Delta variant than fully vaccinated, previously uninfected individuals.[7] The same study found that there was a 27 fold increased risk for symptomatic breakthrough infection in vaccinated individuals compared to reinfection for individuals with natural immunity.[8]

The Israeli studies are not alone in suggesting the potency of natural immunity. Earlier this year, the National Institutes of Health (NIH) published an article about a January 2021 study from the La Jolla Institute for Immunology with the headline "Lasting immunity found after recovery from COVID-19."[9] The article stated that the researchers found that more than 95 percent of those who recovered from COVID-19 had durable immune system memory of the virus

---

[3] Speech by President Joseph R. Biden on COVID-19, Sept. 9, 2021, transcript available at https://www.nytimes.com/2021/09/09/us/politics/biden-vaccine-mandates-transcript.html.

[4] Frequently Asked Questions about COVID-19 Vaccination, CDC, updated Sept. 9, 2021, available at https://www.cdc.gov/coronavirus/2019-ncov/vaccines/faq.html.

[5] Antibody (Serology) Testing for COVID-19: Information for Patients and Consumers, updated May 19, 2021, available at https://www.fda.gov/medical-devices/coronavirus-covid-19-and-medical-devices/antibody-serology-testing-covid-19-information-patients-and-consumers.

[6] Yair Golderg, et al. Protection of previous SARS CoV-2 infection is similar to that of BNT162b22 vaccine protection: A three-month nationwide experience from Israel, Apr. 24, 2021, (preprint) available at https://www.medrxiv.org/content/10.1101/2021.04.20.21255670v1.

[7] Sivan Gazit, et al, Comparing SARS-CoV-2 natural immunity to vaccine-induced immunity: reinfections versus breakthrough infections, Aug. 25, 2021, (preprint) available at https://www.medrxiv.org/content/10.1101/2021.08.24.21262415v1.

[8] *Id.* at 12.

[9] Sharon Reynolds, Lasting immunity found after recovery from COVID-19, NIH Research Matters, Jan. 26, 2021, available at https://www.nih.gov/news-events/nih-research-matters/lasting-immunity-found-after-recovery-covid-19#main-content (referencing Jennifer M Dan, et al, Immunological memory to SARS-CoV-2 assessed for up to 8 months after infection, Jan. 6, 2021, available at https://www.ncbi.nlm.nih.gov/pmc/articles/PMC7919858/).

September 15, 2021
Page 3

up to 8 months later.[10] The article noted that "the results provide hope that people receiving SARS-CoV-2 vaccines will develop similar lasting immune memories after vaccination."[11]

According to the CDC, an estimated 120 million Americans had been infected with COVID-19 as of May 2021.[12] The CDC itself acknowledges that immunity to a virus can occur "through infection with the actual disease (resulting in **natural immunity**)."[13] I was tested for antibodies and found that seven months after having an asymptotic case of COVID-19, my serology is positive for antibodies against SARS-COV-2 at roughly the same level as an individual that has received the Moderna vaccine.[14] My experience seems consistent with the previously mentioned January 2021 study that found immune memory to SARS-CoV-2 lasted up to 8 months after infection.[15] Some researchers and studies have found that natural immunity from COVID-19 could last years or potentially decades.[16]

To better understand Dr. Fauci's, FDA's, and CDC's positions regarding natural immunity from COVID-19, I request the following information:

1. Approximately 20 months into this pandemic, why have U.S. health agencies not fully studied COVID-19 natural immunity?

2. Please explain why Dr. Fauci supports vaccine mandates for all individuals without apparently considering studies that show the effectiveness of natural immunity against the virus.

3. Did Dr. Fauci recommend to study the protection offered by natural immunity prior to President Biden's decision to impose vaccine mandates? If not, why not?

4. Did FDA and CDC consider the January 2021 NIH article titled, "Lasting immunity found after recovery from COVID-19," or other studies on natural immunity, when deciding that individuals, regardless of previous COVID-19 infection, should be vaccinated? If not, why not?

5. Does the FDA and CDC agree with the World Health Organization's statement that "[a]vailable scientific data suggests that in most people immune responses remain robust

---

[10] *Id.*
[11] *Id.*
[12] Estimated COVID-19 Burden, CDC, updated July 27, 2021, available at https://www.cdc.gov/coronavirus/2019-ncov/cases-updates/burden.html.
[13] Vaccines & Immunizations: Immunity Types, CDC, Mar. 10, 2017, available at https://www.cdc.gov/vaccines/vac-gen/immunity-types.htm. (emphasis included in original text).
[14] I compared the results of my serology test to those of an individual who had received the Moderna vaccine. The results showed that the individual who received the Moderna vaccine and I had similar levels of antibodies.
[15] Jennifer M Dan, et al, Immunological memory to SARS-CoV-2 assessed for up to 8 months after infection, Jan. 6, 2021, available at https://www.ncbi.nlm.nih.gov/pmc/articles/PMC7919858/.
[16] Apoorva Mandavilli, Immunity to the Coronavirus May Last Years, New Data Hint, New York Times, Nov. 17, 2020 (updated July 4, 2021), available at https://www.nytimes.com/2020/11/17/health/coronavirus-immunity.html.

and protective against reinfection for at least 6-8 months after infection"?[17] If not, why not?

6. Is the FDA or CDC aware of any adverse events in previously infected individuals that have been vaccinated? Please provide a complete list of these adverse events.

7. How many Americans received a vaccination after having COVID-19? If this data is unavailable, please explain why.

8. Provide the current estimated total number of infections of COVID-19 in the U.S.

9. Do the FDA and CDC dispute the findings of the two Israeli studies cited in this letter? If so, please provide the data that contradict these studies.

10. Provide the estimated number of breakthrough infections in vaccinated persons versus reinfections in previously infected persons.

11. Please explain why "antibody testing is not recommended to determine whether you are immune or protected from COVID-19."[18]

12. Has the FDA or CDC examined the duration of natural immunity compared to vaccine immunity? If not, why not?

Please provide a response no later than September 29, 2021. Thank you for your attention to this urgent matter.

Sincerely,

Ron Johnson
United States Senator

---

[17] Scientific Brief, COVID-19 Natural Immunity, World Health Organization, May 10, 2021, available at https://apps.who.int/iris/bitstream/handle/10665/341241/WHO-2019-nCoV-Sci-Brief-Natural-immunity-2021.1-eng.pdf.

[18] Antibody (Serology) Testing for COVID-19: Information for Patients and Consumers, updated May 19, 2021, available at https://www.fda.gov/medical-devices/coronavirus-covid-19-and-medical-devices/antibody-serology-testing-covid-19-information-patients-and-consumers.

Chapter 10

The Hammer Drops

"If you find yourself in the line of fire, say your prayers, close your eyes, and ask God to accept you."
- Michael S. O'Neil

This came to me while writing this book. I find this statement very profound. I didn't come up with this, of course, God did. As with everything I do these days, God is a huge part. I pray and ask Him to give me guidance on all things. The statement above can be used in many different scenarios, but the obvious scenario I am looking at here is before you meet Him. This next chapter is symbolically the death of many things in my life, and it is my complete and total submissiveness before God. This entire experience has forged me into what I am today, which, at times, was the most excruciating psychological pain I've ever had to endure. I would find myself constantly medicated with alcohol and, later, marijuana. I don't think anyone would fault me for that, considering the pain I endured, as it was all part of the journey.

I had taken some leave in late October, about a month prior to my scheduled departure from Hawaii. Min and I agreed to meet, and she bought a plane ticket to see me. I reserved a room for a few days at a resort on the island. We both had gone through a lot over the last two years, but we soon would be together. I hadn't felt a woman's touch since I left her, and I was longing to be wrapped up in an embrace, as I was so lonely. Unfortunately, Min couldn't make it and had to back out at the last minute. It was just as well, as I found out that by this time, the resort and most if not all, commercial places in Hawaii required proof of vaccination. As things got closer towards the end of my tour, I felt the noose growing tighter and tighter around my neck.

I felt a spiritual battle going on in my mind as well. For three nights in October, I had a recurring dream about a former friend and colleague I worked with. Each night, I pictured meeting with her in a room. I could visualize her face, and it was always the same setting. After seeing her, and seeing her walk away, I would do battle with a dark force, as if I was sword fighting. There's not much I can describe, other than the whole scene being dark, and not much more that I remember, other than I enjoyed kicking the ass of my opponent. I remember waking up with a bruise over my right kidney about the size of a fist, but I never had any dreams like that one since. My pact with God was sealed, and I would do anything by now in His name, no matter what.

Around this time, I received a message from a friend from high school named Joan, whom I was in a chat group with. She wanted to talk to me about going to Korea and the vaccine. Joan was a nurse and had been in the profession for many years. Early on, after the vaccines were placed on the market, Joan quickly noticed major problems and connected the dots when patients came to see her after receiving the vaccines. She quickly attributed the injuries to the effect of receiving the shot. It wasn't long before, knowing what was happening and refusing to be a part of the tomfoolery that Joan resigned. Thank God for Joan and others like her who would sacrifice themselves because of principles.

I called her when I arrived home from work and we talked at length for at least two hours. She told me that she was worried about me going to Korea and that I should come home. She told me that it wouldn't be long before Americans living abroad would be required to take the vaccine in order to enter the US. I told Joan that I was monitoring the situation and that if my situation changed regarding the job front, I would be on the first plane back to the USA mainland. I acknowledged everything she talked about and assured her that the decision I would make would be a "game-time" decision. I just wasn't ready to give everything up before I was forced to do so.

Meanwhile, based on this conversation and reading the tea leaves, I contacted Min and told her the situation. I had talked about everything before to her, but I'm not quite sure if I mentioned the possibility of not coming to Korea. I wanted to keep that far from her mind, and we were so close to finally being reunited. This was to be a second chance in life for both of us. Though I continued the mindset of going to Korea, I called her and told her of the possibility that I might not make it to her. I told her that I was doing everything I could do in the normal transition phase: scheduling my car for shipment, household goods, picking up plane tickets, etc., but I wanted to be forthcoming and let her know because I didn't want her to have any false hope.

It was still the end of October when I came back to work from leave. I think it was mid-week when I returned. Al, my office mate, told me that we didn't need to wear masks anymore after guidance came down from DOD. Honestly, there was so much guidance coming down and so many changes to the previous guidance, that it was difficult to differentiate between what to do and what not to do. We all had been wearing them when more than three of us were huddled in an office together. Our military supervisor came in and mentioned something to Al. After he was finished, he looked over at my corner and said to me, gesturing with the pointed knife hand, "You need to wear a mask," and began to walk out of the room.

I looked at him and replied, "My leave went very well, sir." It was a pretty sarcastic remark, as I only said it to show how callous and uncaring this man was.

He responded by saying, "I've lived on this island for three years, seen every part of it. You don't have to tell me about it."

I later reported this incident to Dan when he had the three civilian co-workers in his office. I considered this action discriminatory, and I felt ostracized. I would later type up a memorandum to record the incident, along with the disparate treatment I received earlier by this man after I stated I wouldn't take the vaccine. I later told Senator Eric Schmitt of Missouri about it, requesting an investigation of misconduct against this officer. I didn't receive any assistance from the senator. I will address that topic later on in this book.

The good news was the soldier would begin leave the next day, so that Thursday and Friday, I would wear a mask in the office because I agreed when talking about it in Dan's office, and then we would go from there. I felt like a slave, however, being the only one in the section required to wear a mask, and it didn't sit well at all with me. After dealing with the psychological mind games of wearing the mask, I decided on Friday to take leave for the rest of the time I was there. I planned on clearing the installation while doing so, and I didn't want to come into our building unless it was absolutely necessary. I needed to take this leave because I wasn't sure what I was going to say or do to this individual for acting the way he did towards me. Beginning November 1, 2021, I started my leave. From now on, I would not need to come into the office for anything unless it was important.

About this same period, Dwayne, another friend in the chat group with fellow high schoolers, told us he was working on an exemption for the vaccine mandate that would cover everything. He was friends with Dr. Eric Nepute in St. Louis, who also had a friend I had been following for a few months during this time. His name was Tom Renz, a Constitutional Law Attorney out of Ohio. I had a chance to meet Tom at the Texas Reckoning Fest in August 2022 and talked with him for a bit, but I will address that later. Just to be clear, that particular time frame was divine, and that chapter will be explosive. Anyway, I listened to Dwayne on Dr. Nepute's show with Mr. Renz talking about the product he finished. The final product was completed with Dr. Nepute and Mr. Renz both giving their Seal of Approval.

That first week of November was a whirlwind. Dan texted me on Tuesday, November 2nd, telling me I needed to submit an exemption for not taking the vaccine. I told him I was working on it and would turn it in as soon as it was completed. Dwayne had sent me a copy that was 11 pages long, and we went back and forth a couple of times to make sure everything was right. I received the final copy on the 3rd, dated for the 4th, to be turned in. To put things in perspective, I had attempted to turn in a religious exemption to Dan a month earlier. Unfortunately, Dan came into my office to discuss why it needed to be changed. Dan was a helicopter pilot in the Marines and a retired Colonel. I considered him a good friend and mentor but couldn't understand why he didn't just take my exemption and turn it in. He had no legal background, and yet he was trying to explain to me in an unrealistic way as to why *he* felt this letter wasn't good enough. I was taking fire from all sides, so to speak, by this time. Of course, there were no other witnesses to corroborate my story.

I texted back and forth with one of the military officers from my office during this time. I liked him, even though our ideologies were opposite, but I don't make it a point to judge someone based on what they believe or who they follow. He was well-meaning, and he didn't want to see me lose my job. So he sent me something he thought would work for me as a religious exemption, telling me his daughter gave it to him. It was the seven tenets of Satanism. *What in the world am I even seeing this for?* I wondered. I didn't say anything but thanked him for thinking of me and immediately deleted that demonic piece from my phone. I wanted no part of that, and honestly, I was completely taken aback by even seeing it. *What kind of a clown world are we living in right now?* I wondered.

Then the unthinkable happened. On Thursday, November 4th, I received an email from the Human Resources section of 8th Army Command. The email was a revision of my original FINAL offer letter. It stated that I must provide physical proof of vaccination upon arrival in Korea or show an exemption letter. There were a couple of problems with showing the letter. One, it hadn't been approved, and most of the exemption letters provided by soldiers were being denied. I had thought long and hard about the whole exemption letter approach, even before receiving this letter. In the end, I was so grateful that Dwayne took the time and effort to do this for me, but I felt compelled to say in the end that my choice was to not put a foreign, unknown, and untested substance into my body and that this decision was between God and me alone. My reasoning was I shouldn't need an excuse not to take the vaccine and I shouldn't be required to take it.

Beyond this, I questioned the legality of the revised statement. Was it legal for the United States Government to unequivocally change a FINAL offer when nowhere in the original FINAL offer did it state that the USG reserved the right to change anything? The only thing I saw that needed to be done was all required vaccinations needed to be completed before the agreement. When my physical was completed, the COVID-19 vaccine was not required. Was this a breach of contract by the federal government after an agreement was made between both parties? I sure think it was.

As I read this email with the revision, I knew there was no turning back. I looked up to the ceiling and whispered, "WHY, God? WHY???" I was heartbroken! I knew what I had to do, but I knew doing so would make my life a living hell. The path to following God is a narrow path, and I was finding out just how narrow the path is. I would have to give up *everything* because I knew that with this decision, I was on my own. I would have to get rid of all of my things, with the exception of a couple of bags of clothes to ship home.

I would have to get rid of all of my furniture, pots and pans, dishes, and everything I had that I couldn't carry. I was about to become homeless and would jump from place to place, motel to motel - one place being downright unhealthy to the point where they should be shut down by the Health Department. I would use whatever I had left in my savings and cash in my 401K I started five years prior to survive. I would not stop paying my ex-wife the monthly $1800 from my pension, and I received some flack for this. However, I decided that in the end, I walked away from the job. This wasn't her fault, and I wasn't going to make her pay for a decision that I made that I knew would affect my outcome negatively. I am a very principled man.

I immediately began planning my return trip to Missouri after being away for more than 30 years. I wasn't going to turn my resignation in until I had everything taken care of, and that window was closing fast. The first thing I did was make an appointment to turn my car in. I had already talked with the company the prior week to get pricing and details since I wasn't sure about anything. I called back and spoke to the same person I'd spoken to prior and was able to schedule an appointment for the next day to turn the car in. It would cost me $2400 out of pocket to ship my car to St. Louis. Once I made that appointment, I worked out a backward plan from the 9th, when I figured I would fly home if everything was set in place.

After turning my car in, I caught an Uber to the airport so I could pick up a rental car. From there, I canceled my household goods and appointments and called to find out how much it would cost to have everything in my apartment picked up. It was Friday the 5th, and they scheduled pickup for Sunday. Once that appointment was set and I knew everything was taken care of, I scheduled a flight to leave on the 9th. I drove over to Pearl Harbor to schedule a two-night stay on November 7th and 8th before turning in my rental car and leaving Honolulu mid-day on the 9th.

I stayed at Pearl Harbor for a few weeks when I first arrived, so I knew I was in good hands. I made the appointment with the desk clerk and obtained my credit card so I could pay for the two nights, when he asked me, "May I see your vaccination card?"

I was mortified, but I kept my composure. "Oh, I don't have it on me," I said.

To which he asked, "It's not on your phone?"

"No," I stated.

"Well, just show it to the desk clerk the day of the 7th when you check in, otherwise, we can't let you stay here," he added.

I walked out, knowing this was not going to end well. I thought of Minh. Just after I thought of him, low and behold, my phone rang and who was it on the other end? None other than Minh. Tell me this isn't God at work because no matter what hell I went through, He was *always* there for me! I told Minh about my situation and that I thought of him immediately after being told about the vaccination card. If it wasn't for Minh, I would be out on the streets the last two days of my time in Hawaii, sleeping in my rental car before flying home. God is great!

With everything being prepared and ready to execute, I took time Saturday morning to go to the office and drop off my office keys and badges for the last time. I opened up my Outlook and began to construct a resignation letter. This letter would be addressed to 8th Army Command IG, the USARPAC Command IG and Deputy IG, with General Charles Flynn, brother of retired LTG Michael Flynn, on the CC line. I have redacted the correct email addresses. The letter is listed below.

* * *

From: "O'Neil, Michael S CIV USARMY USARPAC (USA)" <michael.s.oneil.civ@mail.mil>

Date: November 6, 2021 at 09:00:05 HST

To: "Horine, Brian S COL USARMY USARPAC (USA)" <XXXXXXXXXXXXXX@mail.mil>, "Deamon, Daniel C CIV USARMY USARPAC (USA)" <XXXXXXXXXXXXXX.civ@mail.mil>, "Wood, Warren Ray (Ray) COL USARMY 8 ARMY (USA)" <XXXXXXXXXX.mil@mail.mil>

Cc: "Flynn, Charles A GEN USARMY USARPAC (USA)" <XXXXXXXXXXX.mil@mail.mil>

Subject: The Resignation of Mr. O'Neil (UNCLASSIFIED)

CLASSIFICATION: UNCLASSIFIED

ALCON,

I cannot in good conscience follow an unlawful

order given by an illegitimate president unelected by We the People.

I will not allow an experimental gene therapy in its infancy stage enter into my body without knowledge of long term ramifications of doing so.

Therefore, after long and careful consideration, I have decided to resign from service to the federal government.

I will not allow the State to make the choice that I alone should be determined to make after thoughtful consideration.

My resignation is effective immediately.

It has been my honor to serve, both in uniform, as a contractor in Afghanistan, and now as a Federal Employee.

God Bless and God Speed!

Thanks,

Mike

Mr. Michael S. O'Neil

Department of the Army Civilian

Inspector General

United States Army Pacific

Fort Shafter, HI 96858-5100

I blind copied my friend and former boss, Rob, in Korea. He just so happened to be in his office then (it was Sunday morning, Korea time) doing a couple of things. I received a call from him, and we talked at length. He told me he had received the job to go up to 8th Army to be the deputy but was waiting on movement orders, and the folks were dragging their feet. *There goes my promotion to GS-13, Deputy IG*, I thought. That one hurt because I was working toward becoming a deputy, and things were moving pretty quickly for me in the IG world. Now, this world would go further and further away from me, and I was hurt and upset, but I knew the ramifications of what that vaccine was doing to people, and I had to make a stand. I put everything before God, and I knew this would be a living hell in doing so, but I did it anyway.

Next came contacting Luanna, Nav, and Min. I contacted Min first. It was in a long message. I told her I was sorry that I couldn't make it to see her. I was absolutely heartbroken, even knowing I did the right thing. I don't know exactly how Min felt about me not coming because she was very supportive of me, but knowing how I felt, it had to be very hurtful for her too. After all, this was the second time, and after I left Korea the first time, she took my absence extremely hard. I remember the message Nav sent back to me like it was yesterday. He said, "You don't deserve this!" Even now, I get a bit choked up rehashing all of this, but I absolutely need to remember that all of what I have been through was forging me through fire to make me who I am today.

So, on Sunday, the crew arrived to pick up my belongings. They packed everything I owned up minus what I had already packed and stored, and completed the job in about 2 and ½ hours. As Minh and I were leaving my apartment to go to his place, I noticed a text I received from Dan a few minutes prior. The first part of the text read, "COL Horine told me you put in your resignation. That makes me sad."

Quite frankly, I found it to be a bit disingenuous given our relationship, and I expected a call, but it wasn't to be. I professionally answered him and assured him I had everything taken care of and did not require any assistance. It reminded me of what Trump told Charlie Rose in an interview about loyalty, and I have not forgotten about what transpired that day.

My awareness by now was completely heightened, and when we arrived at Minh's apartment, I went to the room I had stayed in before. Everything suddenly hit me about this room. Looking around, I noticed a picture of the Lion of Judah hanging directly above the bed's headboard. Everything in the room was white including the walls, the bed, *everything*. Minh had a painting titled *View Of The Naruto Whirlpools At Awa,* leaning up against the wall from the floor. I didn't realize it at the time, but the painting was upside down, and it stayed that way until I realized it the next day. I remember looking at it closely while lying in bed, the waves raging in the sea. I couldn't make out what was at the bottom of the painting, so I took a closer look.

As I approached the painting, I noticed something was off with it. I don't know what possessed me to do so, but I turned the picture around. At this point, it all came to me clearly. I was in a storm with waves crashing down on me all at once. It was extremely painful spiritually and psychologically. I learned that this place - the room - was God's refuge. When I turned the right side of the painting up, I saw birds and the sky, and it was beautiful. I was resting in the palm of His hand as He guided Minh and me to turn to each other. The last two days of my time in Hawaii were bliss; I needed it for the long journey ahead.

Finally, on November 9, 2021, I was traveling from Hawaii en route to an uncharted future in a place I hadn't known for decades. I was jobless, homeless, and would receive about $600 monthly from my pension after taxes were taken out, while $1800 was given to my ex-wife. It was two years to the day since I saw Min, and I didn't know when I would see her again. I was moving to the beat of God's drum, with an uncertain future ahead, and I knew things would be tough. I just didn't know how tough life was going to be.

Exempt from Biden's vaccine mandates:

Congress/legislative branch
Congressional staff
Judicial branch
White House staff
CDC employees
FDA employees
USPS employees
NIAID employees
Pfizer employees
Moderna employees
Illegal aliens

Chapter 11

A Sort of Homecoming

My aunt and uncle picked me up at Lambert Airport in St. Louis. Since picking up passengers at this airport is most often a dicey situation with traffic, we agreed I would call them when I arrived at the pickup point outside of the terminal. I remember walking outside and waiting by a sign numbered 17. I will talk about the seventeenth letter often in this second part, as it showed up many times over the length of my journey with the People's Convoy, the time I was connected with Take Action USA, and on my drive home from Biglerville, PA, where I lived and worked at an International Paper box factory for almost one year.

I was extremely grateful that my Uncle Tom and Aunt Diana took me into their home. I had been displaced before. I retired from the Army in 2010 to fill one of the vacant positions in 8th Army IG Office when the job I had counted on filling was reserved for someone else. My family lived with another family that we had been friends with for years over a period of six months. Living with others can be challenging, since they already have their own lives and the rest of the idiosyncrasies that go with it. I found after living with several people over this period that things are not in your control and you must walk a tightrope, because people open their doors to you out of kindness. Nevertheless, the Lord, as always, was looking out for me and He provided me with shelter, and I would be forever grateful.

When I arrived in my hometown after a 32-year absence, I did not recognize many things. Sure, I had been home at least 17 times over that period to visit, but now I would be there permanently, or so I thought. I had to relearn almost everything about the town I grew up in. So many places considered the "sticks" in the 80s were fully built up and thriving, while others, especially in the metropolitan area, lay in decay. I remember riding my bicycle all over the city decades prior and seeing run-down parts of the city then, but now my city was lying in rot. To the west of the city, Fenton was the boundary before getting into the country, and much of Fenton was country. To the south, Arnold was the boundary and similar to Fenton. Traveling further south to Festus was definitely full of country folk. St. Charles was not even close to what it looks like today. A lot of change happens over the course of a generation.

Right before leaving Hawaii, I watched an episode of Dan Bongino, which was dated November 5, 2021. Dan showed a clip of St. Louis District 1 Representative Cori Bush talking about Kyle Rittenhouse, with her totally uninformed opinion regarding the trial. Anyone who followed what happened the night of the shootings knows about the 11-minute video documenting Rittenhouse providing medical aid to the wounded and putting out fires with a fire extinguisher that rioters were attempting to start in dumpsters. That video showed Rittenhouse being bullied by his first attacker, ultimately leading to the felon pedophile's death.

Knowing that time was not on my side, and not having any real money to campaign, I explained to my aunt and uncle that I wanted to make a GO at running against her. I called up the St. Louis County Republican Renee Artman and asked her what I needed to do to get into the race. I noted and mentioned to her that if my phone number had three consecutive 6s in it, I would get a new phone number. She laughed. I only bring this up because of the numbers and the spiritual journey I've been on. I don't know what the numbers mean, but I know this journey is all about the numbers and that everything is connected.

I started by looking at the schedule of the Republican meetings across the county. The first one I went to was the Bridgeton Community Center, located in Midland Township, about three miles west of Lambert Airport. The date was November 23rd, two days before

Thanksgiving, and I remember being quite nervous at the time. Remember that I didn't have a lot of personal interaction with people because of the lockdown, so this was a big step for me. The meeting was to begin at 7:00 pm and I arrived approximately 30 minutes prior. There was no signage anywhere, so I walked freely about the community center, a little fearful to ask questions since I was beginning to feel my anxiety take over. The 7 o'clock hour arrived, and no one was still around, so I waited. I waited until twenty minutes after the hour before I decided to get back in my car and go home. The first night was a bust.

About 10 days later, I traveled to the Bonhomme Township Republican Club Meeting at the American Legion in Kirkwood, Missouri. This meeting, like the one in Midland Township, began at 7:00 pm. Like the previous week, I arrived in Kirkwood early. There were two women, I don't remember their names, setting up the tables and chairs for a Christmas party. I asked if I could do anything to help, and they gladly accepted my assistance. They asked a little bit about me, and I told them. I mentioned my service, my coming home after 30 years, the reason, and what my intentions were.

I told them that in my short time back home, I researched Andrew Jones, the Republican who unsuccessfully ran for St. Louis Mayor twice, who put in the Republican bid for a seat not held by any Republican since 1948. What I noticed that didn't sit well with me was when he declared his candidacy, the poster sitting right by the podium said "Andrew Jones for Mayor." I didn't know this guy, and by no means do I write this out of disrespect, but looking at the followers of his social media accounts, along with two failed bids for office, declaring your candidacy while not displaying the proper optics, quite frankly tells someone like me that you are not doing everything you can to win. When going up against a Soros-backed candidate, one needs to be prepared.

So, when it came time, one of the ladies introduced me to the group of approximately 20 and I gave a 5-6 minute speech of who I was, where I came from, and why I was there. I must have turned some heads because there were a few people who came up and talked to me, while others stood in waiting. One of the individuals who talked to me was running unopposed for a seat in the Missouri House Legislature, named Brad Christ. Brad, I found out belonged to St. Catherine Labore Parish in South County, not far from Lindbergh High School. Many years ago, I went to school at that parish in the 8th grade and was an altar boy at that church.

Brad gave me his number, and I later texted him to thank him for his kind words. He then added one of his consultants to the text, saying we needed to link up because "Mike was the next person to beat Cori Bush." I must have really struck a nerve for him to say something like this, and honestly, it made my night. So I called his consultant, Joe was his name, the next day. We spent close to forty-five minutes on the phone together, and for most of that time, he gave me the impression of why I shouldn't run against Ms. Bush. I must have done something right, though, because by the end of the call, he gave me an appointment to come to his office in Kirkwood, MO, the following week.

So the following Wednesday, at 11:00 am, I arrived at Joe's office for my appointment. There was only one other person in the office at the time. I did not recognize him at the time since I had been away from home so long, but the future Senator Eric Schmitt was there. He was about finished with his business with Joe, stood up, and made eye contact with me while I approached him to shake hands. I'm not sure if he was aware I had no idea who he was. It's pretty funny now as I think about it while I type. Anyway, Joe and I sat down at the table together to talk. Again, he did everything he could to stop me from running. I couldn't figure this out because I gave him the knowledge I had about no Republican holding that seat since '48. I laid out my approach and said that given my background and the things I had experienced, I felt I could go toe to toe with her.

It would require an unconventional campaign, and I was already researching the Counter Intelligence (COIN) operations manual the Army used to win hearts and minds. I would take the fearless approach of taking her head on, and this would require spending time speaking to people with opposing views on the opposite side of the aisle. I could read his body language, his leg shaking in excitement. He grew up rooting for Kurt

Warner, as Kurt's story was a Cinderella story, and I compared that with what could be. He told me how Republicans couldn't stand Cori Bush but that they most likely would not spend the money to go up against her. I took that as being happy with the status quo; maybe something else was going on entirely. He told me that he would think about our conversation and get back with me. I never heard from him again.

I ran into Brad again, along with a few others from the meeting in Kirkwook at Attorney General Eric Schmitt's new office opening party at Gravois Bluffs in Fenton, Missouri. I went there that night with my Aunt Diana, who wasn't sure who to vote for in the primary anyway, so she was interested in hearing what AG Schmitt had to say. Brad and I had a nice chat, and I talked with a few others, some I was already introduced to previously, while others I met for the first time. The office wasn't too big but big enough to give a nice speech. There were probably about 75 people at the opening in total, with plenty of Scmitt giveaways laying on the tables against the wall. Diana and I sat in folding chairs located in the second row in front of the podium and listened to his speech. When he was done, people gathered around him for a more natural setting, with conversation going back and forth. I was going to talk with him, but he was fully engaged in a one-on-one conversation, and we left shortly afterwards.

The next night, December 16th, I headed to the South County Republicans meeting. Brad and I talked about it the previous night at the Scmitt office opening when I asked him if the meeting was still being held. I approached the building about 6:45 pm and rang the doorbell, but there was no answer. I walked around the building, checking doors and windows, which seemed abandoned. When I called Brad to find out what happened, he told me they were currently sitting in the Smoke Shack, which was a restaurant in the area that had good barbecue. Since it was near Christmas, the group met up there to break bread and celebrate.

I arrived about twenty minutes later to a packed house. I felt my anxiety kicking in because of my experience during the lockdowns in Hawaii and the awkwardness I felt going into a place where everyone already was sitting, and I would have to sit on the outside part of the group. I guess there is a good reason for showing up early, which is how I normally conduct myself. I sought out Brad and had a short chat before finding a table to sit down at. I had already eaten dinner, so I was not the least bit hungry, but I took a gander at the menu and ordered a Budweiser from the tap at the bar. A few minutes later, I decided to order *the foxhole*, which came in a wrap. Inside came smoked beef and cheese, with lettuce and onions, jalapenos and bacon bits. While ordering, the server mentioned that this was a popular item on the menu. It definitely did not disappoint, and I ate half of it rather slowly. I would take the other half with me when I left.

After a time, Brad signaled me to work my way

around the room. I was a bit overwhelmed, but I began to make my rounds. I started at one of the side tables to introduce myself and tell my story. I didn't want to mention that I was homeless, of course, and technically, I had a roof over my head, so I wasn't, and I wasn't looking to play the victim either. I moved a bit from table to table, talking with some nice folks. There were a couple of questions, such as where I lived and if I had a website to look at.

I was completely unprepared, but I pushed on the best I could. Close to the end of the night, I engaged in conversation with one of the Missouri State Representatives and Brad. Again, Brad introduced me as "the next man to beat Cori Bush." I was pretty impressed with his enthusiasm. No one else had shown this enthusiasm, and I was extremely grateful to him for doing so. This wasn't the first time he had mentioned that for this to be successful, outside money - money from outside of Missouri - would be necessary for me to compete against the Soros-backed candidate.

I don't remember the name of the gentleman I spoke with, but he instructed me that if I wanted outside money, I needed to go directly to Washington, D.C. and request it. I thought to myself, "Wow, all I need to do is go to Washington, D.C., knock on the door, and say Hi! I'm Mike O'Neil, and I want to take on Cori Bush. Will you give me some money?" I was really taken aback, because I was genuinely interested in going up against her, knowing my background and experiences would give me a boost, but I was not being taken seriously. I talked with Brad a bit later one-on-one and told him I wasn't giving up, and he applauded me for that. My biggest obstacle would be time and money, neither of which I had.

This was the last event I would go to. A couple of days later, I fell ill and was confined to my bedroom. During the Christmas season, the Omicron variant of COVID-19 was spreading, getting people sick. I don't know if I caught it or not, but I was down for the remaining part of December. I didn't have the normal symptoms of fever, loss of smell or taste, or nausea. I just felt light-headed, lacked energy, and, for the most part, did not have an appetite for the first few days. To be on the safe side, I stayed in my room most of the time, unless my aunt and uncle were not home, and that happened rarely. I remember at the halfway point of my sickness I went to the kitchen to get something to eat and immediately went back upstairs because I felt very dizzy. I spent the entire Christmas isolated in my bedroom and only felt better just before New Year's.

I was still in bed when I began searching the internet for jobs. I came across an administrative position for a local company I'd not heard of named the McAfee Institute. Almost immediately after applying, I received a phone call. On the other end of the call was Chris, who told me he looked at my resume and thought I would be more interested in another position because of my military background. After the phone call ended,

I received a job description for Director of Military Admissions. I read over the description, was pretty impressed with the responsibilities of the job, and decided to give it a try. So, after an interview with Josh McAfee, the CEO of McAfee Institute, I scheduled a face-to-face interview in front of a panel and was hired. The position would begin the following week. I messaged Brad to let him know I had found a new position and that I would not be pursuing anything further with a possible campaign.

Before beginning at McAfee Institute, my Uncle Tom and I talked at length about the living arrangement. We both agreed that with my accepting a position at McAfee Institute, I would need to be on my own. So I packed all my belongings, minus the two unopened boxes my ex-wife sent from the house and a couple of bags I had sent from Hawaii, and stored them in my car. I thanked them both for giving me shelter for the time being, and moved into a hotel a very short distance from where the institute was located, with the intent on looking for a place to rent as soon as I had the chance to do so. The long roller coaster ride of my life would only get more interesting from here, and each chain of events would open the door to another. It would not always be fun, but I know it was destined.

Chapter 12

A New Journey

For many years, I have held the belief that certain people come into our lives for a reason, a predestined plan, so to speak, to help guide us along in our journey. Some of the people we come across become part of our lives for a season, while others become a part of a longer term. Regardless of the period in time, I believe these puzzle pieces in our lives which God brings together, forge us into who we are based upon the experiences we live together. I believe the next phase in this journey was a stepping stone into something more that would bring me closer to God.

It was the beginning of January 2022, and I moved into a Comfort Inn & Suites motel not far from where I was hired by Josh McAfee, Owner and CEO of McAfee Institute. Hired as the Director of Military Admissions, I would be challenged like I hadn't been challenged before. After all, I had never heard of McAfee Institute, and as I quickly found out, I would need to give much more than 100 percent to succeed. There were three of us in training, and from the very first day, I felt the pressure mounting to spend most of my time outside of class learning the material. Staying on at McAfee was not a given, and after my experience with leaving a job I loved and everything behind, I felt the pressure mount because I needed that source of income.

At that point in time, McAfee Institute taught mainly online certifications to military, law enforcement, and intelligence specialists in seventeen areas (not all inclusive), such as investigative training, cyber crime, open source intelligence, loss prevention, human trafficking and crypto currency investigations. The two-week training period was brutally demanding, and I wasn't sure if I was going to make it through. I stayed up late at night and studied the material covered earlier and reviewed the material already covered. At the end of each week, we were tested on the knowledge we learned. At the end of the day, I think what pulled me through was not giving up, which I wanted to do at one point.

There were a couple of counseling sessions I had with Josh where I poured out my soul. I wasn't ready to do something like this because I was still an emotional wreck from my experience in Hawaii. I continued to study, however, and with a little bit of tutelage from Josh and Chris, his Director of Operations, I made it through some of the most intense mental training I had ever experienced. I was now ready to continue on in my new position and establish relationships with military counterparts in an effort to bring quality training to the ranks.

Working at McAfee Institute established an interesting dynamic in my life. Getting to know and sell the business was difficult since I had never been able to keep up with new technology and had a hard enough time keeping up with existing technologies. Knowing Josh, however, brought an interesting aspect to my life. During our off time, he invited his employees to meet some of the friends in his circle. One of his friends I cherished meeting and getting to know was Ann Dorn. We first met at a restaurant in downtown St. Louis called Carmine's Steakhouse. The first night we met, we sat next to each other and had a wonderful conversation. I think Josh may have been trying to set us up, and I would be open to something like that, but I was totally committed to God and what He had planned for me. Still, we had a couple of nice evenings together.

We next met at the Backstoppers Ball, a formal gathering held with a group of first responders who raise money to help eliminate the debt of surviving family members of first responders who die in the line of duty, along with covering insurance fees, out of pocket medical costs, tuition and educational costs, etc. Ann and I enjoyed a few dances together and the night overall was exquisite. During my time at McAfee, we would meet three times, and months later, after my time with the People's Convoy, I would approach her for a position in an organization I was a part of.

I worked at McAfee Institute for about six weeks in total. Truthfully, I was way over my head trying to sell a product I was still learning about. Josh is the type who can visualize in his mind what he wants. His resume is rather impressive, as not only was he in law enforcement, but he studied under the tutelage of author John C. Maxwell and worked as a Vice President of Amazon under Jeffrey Bezos. I had already known for a couple of weeks that it was only a matter of time before the inevitable happened. Josh and I had that difficult conversation one Tuesday afternoon. I completely broke down while talking to Josh, knowing this wasn't the right fit for either of us. I had given my all and then some, but it wasn't good enough. My lack of knowledge in the field of technology, coupled with my lack of confidence with the material inevitably led to the realization I needed to move on. We both agreed to move on and then shook hands.

Again, without a job, I received assistance from Josh's Director of Operations, Chris. Through Chris, I found a long-term motel I could stay in that I could afford for the time being until I found a job and could get back on my feet. The Woodspring Suites in Arnold, Missouri, was the place I would reside. It was a pretty decent place overall and definitely better than some motels I would find myself in. It was in a shopping center with a few restaurants and a grocery store, so I was okay for the time being with the funds I had in my bank account.

With much free time on my hands, I tried to figure out what I wanted to do. By the end of the month, I would turn 51 and not have the slightest clue as to what I wanted to do, as I was boxed in with my years of military and government service. I was listening to one of my podcasts and learned of a trucker convoy that would begin in Adelanto, California and end up in Washington, D.C. This protest came on the heels of the trucker protest against the tyrannical COVID-19 vaccination mandates that the Canadian government imposed on its citizens. Since I had left my government job over the vaccine mandates, I felt the need to participate. The convoy would pass through St. Louis, but I had other plans.

So, on the morning of Saturday, February 26th, I set out on a spiritual journey moving east, leaving most of my possessions in the hotel, thinking it would only be a couple weeks before I would return. I was a few days ahead of the convoy, but I needed to venture out on my own before meeting up somewhere. I drove east through Illinois. I wasn't sure where this trip would lead me prior to meeting up with the convoy, but I knew that I needed to just let go and let God take over. My mind felt as if it was flying while driving on Interstate 70. I drove at a steady pace and let my mind go. I stopped in Columbus, Ohio the first night but couldn't get out of bed the next day, so I stayed another day there. The strange piece of this journey was that I would reach very high highs but then I would come crashing down. So, it was not uncommon for my anxiety and depression to kick in after feeling spiritual bliss.

Late morning on February 28th, I set out from Columbus and drove south on Interstate 65 until I reached Nashville, Tennessee. I didn't stop to look at any of the sights, however, because I was just in a driving mood. From Nashville, I drove east on Interstate 40, where I ended up in Knoxville, TN, and stayed there another two days. I have no idea why, other than it being part of God's plan, but I reached out to my long-time friend and former army commander, Rob. Rob had experienced some hardships himself after leaving the army a few years earlier. We had kept in touch over the years, but I hadn't seen him since we were both in Dubai in 2013.

Rob was currently living in Pennsylvania near Gettysburg with his mom. He was working at a Chewy's factory in Mechanicsburg, about an hour's drive from where he lived. He worked nights but was off after he came home the morning of the next day. We agreed to meet, so on the morning of March 2nd, about 11:00 am, I set off towards Pennsylvania. When I arrived that evening, Rob had steaks ready for the grill and plenty of Yuengling beer to drink. We stayed up all night and drank the 30-pack he'd bought and the rest of whatever he had in the downstairs refrigerator. We hashed out old-time memories, both good and bad, and he told me about the job he was working at Chewy's and how physically demanding it was for someone his age.

I met Rob's mom for the first time since he was my commander nearly 20 years previous, and I hadn't remembered whether or not we had met when she visited Rob in California, but we talked about it and came to the conclusion that we had indeed met briefly. She was very proud of her son, and it showed. I would later discuss the close relationship she had with her son and how I had wished the relationship between my mother and me would have been close like it was between those two.

We slept for most of the day until Rob had to leave for work in the early evening. I had planned on driving back west to meet up with the convoy in Ohio, where I would meet up with a longtime army buddy named Arvid. Rob and I agreed it best that I stayed a second night, and then meet up with the convoy as they traveled through Ohio. So, the night after I arrived, Rob worked while I conversed with Karen, his mom, and watched television. The morning of March 4th, when Rob came home from work, Karen cooked a good bacon and scrambled egg breakfast for the both of us. I enjoyed this time with my friend and his mom because I did not know when we would see each other next. Rob and I gave each other a hug, and I left the house in my car en route to the People's Convoy, traveling now on Interstate 70 through Ohio. An exciting new adventure lay in the wings, and it would produce some long-lasting friendships.

Chapter 13

The People's Convoy

A few hours after leaving Rob's, I took an exit off of I-470, where at least 100 people gathered on an overpass in Eastern Ohio. My army buddy Arvid and his friend had met up with the convoy the night before in Cambridge, Ohio. I had been in contact with him by phone while driving, and Arv let me know that the convoy had a late start that morning. I couldn't help but feel a deep sense of love and patriotism walking around on the overpass. There were so many people standing on this bridge waving their American flags and self-made signs to show their support for the truckers and many others who joined in with the convoy. I witnessed a guy on guitar playing his music for the people. The air was filled with love and hope on this sunny early spring morning.

About twenty minutes after my arrival, looking off into the distance, the first vehicles of the convoy appeared. Everyone began cheering, and those who sat in their vehicles began honking their horns. It was a magnificent sight to see so many trucks with their lights flashing and their horns honking as they passed by the overpass. Soon after, Recreational Vehicles (RVs) passed under as they honked and waved. There were flags of many different kinds, many of which were pro-Trump. I found out quickly, there were people of many different political backgrounds who joined in on this march for freedom against the government and medical tyranny bestowed upon the American population, and that of the world for that matter.

Once the RVs drove past the overpass, I walked over to my vehicle and prepared to jump in with the convoy. Once I identificated Arv and Shawn as they passed, I sped onto the highway and caught up to Shawn's box truck, which was traveling behind Arv. We continued the trek through the rest of Ohio, West Virginia, Pennsylvania, and Maryland. Each time we passed a major bridge along the route, we were greeted by large groups of patriotic Americans standing atop, cheering us on with flags and signs. It was so heartwarming to see them jumping, dancing, and waving up there all while we drove by. Even when we were in the middle of nowhere there were at least a couple of patriots showing their support of the convoy up on a bridge or out to the side of the exit. I can only imagine what it felt like to make the whole trek across the country from Adelanto, CA to see the support from the bridges the entire length of the country.

By the time we pulled off of Interstate 81 in Hagerstown, MD it was dark. I was unaware then, but the marshaling point was the Hagerstown Speedway. Being near the rear of the convoy, we were not aware what was happening towards the front. Arv, Shawn, and I pulled into a Sheetz gas station not far from the speedway. None of us knew how much further the speedway was, and since the logjam of vehicles was not moving, we contemplated where to stay that night. There were cars full of people moving in the opposite direction, with a few of them telling us that officials were not letting in any more people. Thankfully, we decided to press on and got back into the line of traffic moving toward the speedway.

Finally, we arrived at Hagerstown Speedway more than two hours after exiting the freeway. We were directed towards the back end of the lot, and vehicles of all types and sizes were parked in many different areas in an orderly fashion. I remember getting out and having a conversation with Arv and Shawn, whom I'd met for the first time. Arv and I hadn't seen each other in more than twenty years, so this was a much welcomed reunion. He and Shawn wasted no time getting the barbecue grill out to cook some burgers and brats. Arv also brought some homemade beer he had brewed on his farm. That turned out to be a late night, as the food was cooked, the music played, and the beer was consumed.

That night, we met Davy, a trucker who owned a teal colored rig from Colorado. The three of us all warmed up to Davy, who was a very down-to-earth guy and was totally dedicated to this fight. We would have quite a few more encounters with Davy, even though after the first night, the three of us were instructed to move to a different spot because the organizers planned on staging more trucks in the area where we parked.

We received word early Saturday morning that there would not be any trip to the D.C. beltway on Saturday. This allowed time for everyone to get settled in and for the organizers to find volunteers to help set up and make logistical plans for the large following. This also allowed time for us to find a better spot to set up camp. We moved our three vehicles up closer to the edge of the speedway parking lot near a hill where the woods began. This was a nice tucked away spot away from large crowds. We parked near a man from Washington who had brought along 42-foot River Ranch RV hooked up to the back of his Ford F-Series Third Wheel and Harley Davidson motorcycle in tow. There were others close in that area, but we seemed to set a nice perimeter around the immediate vicinity, especially since an abandoned flatbed trailer and two empty tractor trailers next to his RV gave us an additional boundary area so we could have nice private campfires away from the larger groups.

Up on the main stage during the day on Saturday, people were allowed to randomly come up and talk, many giving a glimpse into their private struggles resulting from the vaccine mandates. I looked around to see that many people brought their entire families. I knew how important it was to stand up against these tyrannical mandates based on complete lies, but it was heartwarming to see many people from different backgrounds joining in this fight. Throughout the first day, many spoke to the crowd in the speedway stands about what these mandates were doing to the regular people who were just doing what they could to get by. As Doctor Paul Alexander spoke about what this vaccine was doing to people and shouted, "LOCK THEM UP!" I couldn't help but notice the journalists positioning themselves like vultures with their cameras clicking away at everyone in the crowd. I wouldn't be surprised if this was done in order to put everyone there on some type of watch list.

Later on that day, while walking around the parking lot, I stopped by a table of Chinese Americans, who brought a large amount of Chinese food from a local restaurant in support of the protesters. I talked with one of the ladies, who told me this group was at the J6 protests in support of Donald Trump after the stolen election. She told me she couldn't understand why the media lied so much. She said that she left China to get away from Communism, and yet she could see the media in the US being run by the State. We both embraced each other and cried at what we both witnessed taking place. I was moved most of all by this particular group because they knew more than anyone what was at stake for America since they escaped Communist China.

The main coordinator and face of the People's Convoy was Brian Brase, a trucker from Ohio who held briefings to the followers twice each day; the first usually around 7:00 am and the last around 8:00 pm. Brian was the right speaker for the time. He knew how to get a crowd going with his motivational speeches. His rallying cry would be "THEY WORK FOR US!" and the crowd would love it! On Saturday evening, Brian addressed the crowd to let us all know that we would travel to Washington D.C. the next morning, Sunday, March 6th. Brian made it clear that for the first few times, we would circle the D.C. beltway. I can only estimate that this was to ease everyone in on the way to the capital instead of facing the same tyranny the Canadian truckers faced in Ottawa.

So that next morning, after the morning briefing, those participating in the drive mounted up and awaited their turn to roll out of the speedway. It took around 30 minutes after the first trucks departed before we moved our vehicles. The order of march was the semi trucks, followed by RVs and all others. All along the route, every time we passed by a bridge, large crowds were there to greet us, waving their flags and cheering us on. Even though I was in the strange position of not having a job or a place to call home, I felt as free as one could be. I didn't have to answer to anyone and it was during these times that I felt bliss among a sea of sadness. We circled the capital twice that day, slowing traffic around the beltway since there were so many of us. Normally, I hated driving in traffic, but this was different. We were letting the people of D.C. know we were here. I only remember one bridge filled with anti-convoy goers, and all they did was show their Biden signs, but it didn't bother anyone since they were peacefully protesting against what we were doing.

Arv had to be back home on Sunday, so he followed the convoy along the beltway and departed the D.C. Beltway en route to Ohio and we returned to Hagerstown. It was terrific to catch up with my friend, as we first met in Germany more than 30 years ago, and we still keep in touch today. Shawn was able to stay a while longer, so he and I hung together over the next week. When we arrived back in Hagerstown, we stopped off at an AC&T gas station to top off our fuel tanks and get whatever we needed from the store inside. While waiting for Shawn, I sat at a table outside, opened Facebook, and decided to do a live feed detailing the day's events. I owned an iPhone XR, which was already outdated technology since all new cell phones possessed three camera lenses to my one. I gave a short summary, probably no more than two minutes in length, but this would be the beginning of many livestreams I conducted between Hagerstown and California. It wouldn't be long before I picked up a few freedom loving friends interested in watching my recordings of the convoy.

The next day, Shawn and I decided to drive the beltway together. He borrowed an old box truck from a friend, and we drove it in the convoy. It was an old, raggedy truck, but it had character. The cab of the truck looked somewhat of a European-style cab, and the back literally looked like a box. The back was black and white, and the design looked like white flames. Shawn had placed a banner across the front bumper showing American flags on both sides of the word "FREEDOM." Two smaller American flags were attached to the driver and passenger side mirrors. He had a CB radio in his truck and was monitoring traffic, but the range on his radio wasn't very strong, and his messages were not getting through.

While on the road, we noticed that we were being boxed in by pickup trucks and a white panel van with all kinds of marker writing. It also had an upside-down American flag, signaling a nation in distress. We couldn't figure out why we were being boxed in so that we could not move towards the front, and Shawn was getting visibly upset. We heard traffic over the radio talking about a box truck that had infiltrated the convoy and was thought to be creating havoc for everyone. At first, neither one of us caught on, but after a period of trying to make our way forward and hearing CB traffic talk about keeping the box truck away from the convoy, we realized they were talking about us. Shawn tried unsuccessfully to relay the message over the radio that we were a part of the convoy, but the message didn't come through clearly. This day was not a good day for us traveling the beltway, and Shawn would deal with the source immediately upon return to Hagerstown to clear everything up. Upon arrival at the raceway, we parked the truck in our spot. Shawn took off to find the man driving the white panel van. I don't remember exactly what I was doing, but I had to take care of something quickly and followed Shawn a few minutes later.

As I walked up to the van, Shawn was having a good conversation with the driver. He introduced himself as Curtis and apologized for the earlier mix-up. Apparently, since the truck Shawn drove was old, it did not have much power to keep up with the convoy, especially driving up hilly terrain. Curtis mentioned that since this was happening, a group thought we were purposely trying to spread the vehicles apart. We all exchanged sides of the story on what happened from each point of view that day and had a few laughs. Curtis introduced Shawn and me to some of his buddies, and all was good. From then on, we decided to take my Camry so we wouldn't have any issues like we did that day. The one exception to that rule was on March 10th, when we decided to let the convoy go, and we drove to an exit off of I-81 to set up and cheer the convoy on as it returned from Washington DC. I remember standing next to the truck on the side of the road, standing at the position of attention and rendering a hand salute for at least 45 minutes as the long line of vehicles passed by en route back to Hagerstown.

Earlier that morning, at the morning briefing, Brian introduced Senator Ted Cruz to the crowd. Ted was to ride in the lead vehicle as the convoy drove inside the beltway to the capital. Senator Cruz spoke for a few minutes before handing the microphone back to Brian. We had already seen the meeting of Sens. Cruz and Johnson with the People's Convoy organizers recorded a couple of days prior, as it was livestreamed by one of the convoy members. I was a big follower of Senator Cruz, but quite frankly, I lost a lot of respect for him after witnessing his political grandstanding. I felt Senator Johnson asked some good pertinent questions and gave genuine support, but I knew he would show some type of support against the vaccine mandates after reading the letters he sent speaking out against the vaccines to the various agencies. Mr. Cruz, I felt, wanted to play political football with people's lives and used the People's Convoy as a prop to say he was against the mandates. What those of us within the convoy wanted to see was action, but Cruz did nothing more than to blame Democrats, saying that the Republicans were the minority in Congress. I felt that excuse was a complete copout, and I never looked at Senator Cruz in the same light again.

Shawn and I discussed going to the Trump rally held in Florence, South Carolina, on March 12th and finally decided to go after leaving with the convoy on

March 11th. We decided to leave the convoy from D.C. and head south. Before heading out, we mentioned to Tony, the owner of the River Ranch RV parked next to us, that we would return sometime on the 13th, and I asked him to look after my car while we were away. So, just as Arv left the convoy at the beltway, we did a similar move and drove south. We weren't the only ones going from the convoy, as we saw others driving south towards South Carolina as well. It took us about seven hours to get to Florence, where we spent the night in the truck on the grounds, and Shawn cooked bacon and eggs for breakfast the next morning.

The atmosphere was electric, with people of all ages in attendance. For as far as the eye could see, Trump supporters of all different races and creeds were in attendance in South Carolina. The experience was so fun, and Shawn and I were ushered close to the stage, where we sat in the bleachers behind Trump on his left-hand side. The speech lasted about an hour, I think, since a cold front came through. It had been warming up on the East Coast that week, but during this day, the temperature dropped low enough that you could see people leaving as the speech progressed. I remember leaving as he was finishing up his speech. The temperature must have dropped 30 degrees from the daylight hours.

When we arrived back at the truck, we discussed our options as to whether to stay overnight or get back on the road immediately. We both opted for the latter choice and got back on the interstate for the long drive that would get us back sometime in the middle of the night. I struggled to stay awake to help Shawn as he drove, but he was okay and could make it without me being awake. A little more than halfway through, though, he couldn't go anymore and pulled into a rest stop. We slept there for a few hours before returning to the freeway en route to Hagerstown. When we arrived in the morning, snow blanketed the speedway. Shawn would later gather his belongings and go back to Ohio, where he tended horses. We had a nice time hanging out together, but he had to get back to work and could no longer afford to be away. As for me, it was getting quite clear at this point that I was staying with the convoy. I had no idea how long I would stay, but I wasn't spending a whole lot of money, given the many donations that came in and all of the volunteers that worked in the kitchen for us all. I called the motel where my belongings were and added another month to my plan.

FALL
We the People

FREEDOM
CONVOY
2022
HONK FOR FREEDOM
#FREEDOMCONVOY2022

No More
PLANdemic!

Chapter 14

A Chink in the Armor

As time went on in the convoy, the natives, so to speak, were getting restless. Rumors began to fly regarding the money coming into the convoy, along with drama happening resulting in members of the convoy being kicked out. People had issues with obtaining refunds for gas with the turning in of their gas receipts, rumors were flying that the money handlers were mishandling the money, and most of all, there was a growing number of people who wanted to go into D.C. and remain there like the Canadian truckers did in Ottawa. It was obvious to me, being a military man, that this convoy needed to set up a structure if it was going to survive; otherwise, it would find itself in disrepair.

After my return from South Carolina, the RV owner, Tony, offered me a place to sleep at night, so I wouldn't be sleeping in my car. At first, I declined, wanting to give up what was offered to me to someone else with a greater need. A few minutes later, however, after giving it some serious thought, I reconsidered and accepted. I figured that God was giving me an upgrade in my surroundings, so it would be foolish to turn down the offer that was given to me. Tony had another person staying in his RV named Joel. I grew very fond of Joel and found him comfortable to be around. His political leanings were definitely left, but I've always gravitated towards liberals, even though my political ideology goes totally against most liberal beliefs.

My thought on the subject was that as long as we kept political discussion at bay, we could hang out with anybody. Joel was not part of the liberal status quo, and he led the charge for Bernie Sanders in California during the 2016 primaries against Hillary Clinton. He was an interesting fellow who was originally sent to cover the convoy as it left Adelanto. Sometime during the trek east, he ran into Tony, I think in Arizona, where Tony gave Joel some assistance of some type on the side of the road. It didn't take long for Joel to become a convert, so he went from being a journalist, to an activist protester in favor of freedom against the tyrannical mandate.

Tony was an ordained pastor who felt a higher calling to join the convoy. He and his wife Melissa hail from Washington state, where he ran a used car lot. They are both Patriots who love their country, and they were both proud to take part in this nationwide protest against these illegal medical mandates. Melissa left shortly after the arrival at Hagerstown but would rejoin Tony as the convoy traveled west back to California. I would stay with Tony for the duration as the convoy headed back to California.

On March 15th, I was pleasantly surprised when I received a message on Facebook Messenger from someone halfway around the world. The organizer of the Global Freedom Movement Group page noticed the livestream videos I was posting. His name was Scott Russell, and he had quite a following. It didn't take long before we communicated together as I was driving through the car wash down the road from the speedway. The call came through at about 7:55 pm, and we talked for about 15 minutes. Scott thanked me for doing the livestream and told me who he was. He explained that the following week, he and a group of followers planned on going to the US Embassy in Canberra, Australia, to show support for the truckers. He asked me to give his information to Brian Brase and if Brian would do a video message in support of the citizens of Australia and New Zealand. He also gave me administrative access to his site and requested that I add the Global Freedom Movement Group page to be included in my livestreams as they happened. I was happy to oblige him.

When I returned to the speedway, I immediately sought Brian out. It was sometimes very difficult to find Brian, as he was an extremely busy man. His headquarters was a large red tour bus located near the main stage.

This was where all of the planning was conducted by organizers, so you can imagine how often visitors showed up. He was somewhere on the speedway, so I had to wait quite a while before he returned to the bus. When he did so, I let him know what I had encountered with Scott. So, within a day or so, a connection between Brian and Scott was made, and they conducted a live meeting that Scott posted on his Facebook page. Brian also pre-recorded a message for Scott to give to fellow Australians and New Zealanders to help provide them with hope in their own struggle against the tyrannical mandates and actions against citizens' rights perpetrated by these governments. He would then mention on stage to the convoy about what Australia and New Zealand were doing and gave a strong show of support with roars from the crowd as the speech was livestreamed over Scott's Facebook page.

For the first time since leaving the federal government a few months prior, I felt a sense of accomplishment. I felt that I was a part of something much bigger in life. I know that others felt this way as well, as God had a hand in this movement. It was not without controversy, however, and those not quite in tune may not always see the bigger picture in play. With 21 years of previous military experience, coupled with five years living overseas in austere environments in Afghanistan, I felt the turmoil slowly brewing among the many who were a part of this convoy. This convoy needed a structure in place to survive the road ahead. I mentioned this to Tony and Joel a few times because I noticed the command was taking on too much responsibility, which, in turn, led to lapses in communication with the dedicated following. This movement needed to have different tiers of leadership to keep the lines of communication open. Otherwise, rumors would fly, and the message, therefore, would become convoluted.

That weekend, approximately March 18th, Brian took a weekend trip to be with his family in Ohio. A lot of folks in the camp were getting restless, many of whom wanted to travel to D.C. and stay there, much like what happened with the Canadian Trucker Convoy in Ottawa, Canada, where they set up camp at the capital. Rumors were already flying about shoddy bookkeeping with the incoming donations, along with drama resulting in members of the convoy being kicked out. I kept my nose out of this, as I wasn't making it my business, but people had legitimate concerns that given the right structure, would be answered if the convoy showed more transparency. Things would come to a head late in the evening on March 20th.

Earlier that evening, my former Afghani interpreter, Sharif, showed up in Hagerstown with a couple of Afghani friends, one of whom I had already known when I knew Sharif in Afghanistan. Qasim left Afghanistan a few months prior to Sharif with a Special Immigrant Visa and settled in Harrisburg, PA. Sharif followed not long after. I had conversed with both of them a few years prior and told them of my fondness of Pennsylvania when I lived there recruiting for the Army at the turn of the century. The three Afghans treated us to an authentic Afghan meal I so fondly remembered from when I lived in Mazar-e Sharif, in northern Afghanistan. They brought everything, including the grill to cook the chicken skewers. My new friends were treated to a traditional Afghan meal consisting of chicken, Afghan bread, and my favorite part, consisting of long grain Afghan rice with lamb. There was enough food to feed about ten people, so a few folks who weren't part of our small group were treated as well.

After dinner was eaten, we placed some fresh logs of wood in the fire pit and started a fire. As the fire raged, we joyfully sang songs and told different stories into the night. The three Afghans won the hearts and minds of my new friends, and everybody had a great time. At one point, Sharif called our friend in Afghanistan, whom I advised so many years ago. From 2015 to 2017, I advised an Afghan Brigadier General, with whom I became a close friend. I spent almost every day advising him on the IG duties. It was so good to hear the General's voice after all these years. Just like before, Sharif translated for both of us. The General was living at his home in Panjshir, Afghanistan. I remember him telling me many stories of his home. Qasim talked to him for a bit as well. I was so happy Sharif called him, as it made the entire evening a fond memory I would always hold dear to my heart.

At about 10:00 pm that night, we received word of

an emergency meeting regarding the trip to D.C. the next day. I wasn't aware of this at the time, but a group of military veterans were very upset at the lack of leadership and transparency from the organizers. We walked down to the meeting place and found a few people I wasn't familiar with talking about strategy. I had a difficult time with this because I felt the leadership didn't sanction it, and I wanted no part of something such as this. It turned out, though, that this action brought forth a dialogue. The Afghans and I walked back up to the campsite, and they packed up everything, and we said our goodbyes. Sharif left an additional pot of Afghan rice for me that I took up to Tony's RV and placed into the refrigerator. I thanked them, gave them all hugs, and they departed.

The next morning, Tony told me he stayed at the meeting until it concluded about three hours after it began. He told me that the meeting produced some pretty decent results. In the end, he talked with Grey Wolf, a trucker named Ron, who had prior service in the Air Force. Grey Wolf wasn't actually in the leadership, but he was always around them and was an influencer. Tony mentioned to Grey Wolf the need for an organizational structure model that I had been mentioning over the past few days. Tony told me that Grey Wolf asked him to come up with something to present, so we sat outside at a table in the sun and began working on a structural diagram. We had plenty of time to work on it that day since there were no plans to take the convoy to D.C.

Later that evening, Mike Landis, who filled in for Brian on stage while he was gone, gave an update on the next day's events. He briefly touched on what happened the night before and did his best to keep everything from imploding. He gave notice to all veterans in the convoy that there would be a meeting among vets afterwards at the dining area outside of the kitchen. I didn't get a full count, but it looked like there were between fifty to sixty people there. The main theme that came up over and over was the necessity to provide better leadership. Towards the end, somebody talked about the need for some type of structure. This was when I chimed in and talked about the plan I had been working on. I mentioned the necessity of tiered leadership, with the organizers at the top and leaders within each section, such as Semis, RVs, cars, and other miscellaneous groups by type. Each leader would need to cross-talk with other leaders across the convoy to establish confidence among the rest of the group while getting a pulse of trending behaviors and communicating whatever rumors were going around to the leadership to be addressed.

The leaders would engage those in their group daily with information from the leadership team and quash any rumors that might come up. There would be a need for a communications team that would communicate regularly with the head shed and the leaders of each group so information would flow up and down in an orderly fashion. The daily addresses in the mornings and evenings would still be an integral part of this movement, as these people needed to hear a motivating voice like Brian's to keep them from feeling any sense of defeat these mandates brought to them and their families.

The communications team would also conduct investigations of misconduct prior to decisions being made to kick people out of the group, as was happening. I could help with this, given my investigative background as an IG. The tiers of leadership didn't need to look exactly like I had explained, but something close to what I mentioned was necessary. This was the meeting where I met "Liberty" Lauren, who remains a friend today. More on Lauren later, as I would visit her and her beautiful family in West Virginia while I lived in Pennsylvania.

Tony and I continued to work on this project, and I used my lackluster technology skills to complete a PowerPoint presentation to assist in communicating the plan to Mike, Grey Wolf, and Marcus Sommers. Tony and I presented our plan internally to Joel and two others. By now, there were five of us in total hanging around. Boyd had already been hanging around Tony for as long as I can remember, but I hadn't engaged with him very much until this point. Boyd was a handyman who could fix just about anything. He was a farmer from Wisconsin and he was extremely upset at what happened in his state on the night of the election. He was a good man, and I got to know him well later. We met Rebecca for the first time the night our Afghan friends showed up. She wandered over and enjoyed the company at the fire. Rebecca was a special character, as the room usually lit up whenever she entered it. She was a unique part of our group, giving us an interesting dynamic.

The next day as the rain poured down, Tony and I presented the plan to Mike and Marcus, with Grey Wolf in attendance as well. We were located under a large tent near the main stage that was recently set up for dining purposes since the tables outside of the kitchen could not shield us from adverse weather conditions. Brian had just returned from visiting his family and could not make the meeting, but by the end, the organizers seemed to agree the plan could work. Tony and I left the meeting feeling very confident of what we presented. Unfortunately, though, the plan never came to fruition, and to this day I am not sure why, other than it may have been presented unsuccessfully to Brian.

On the evening of March 26th, after a cold and snowy day with speeches to the faithful by Dr. Robert Malone, inventor of the mRNA technology and Dr. Paul Alexander, regarding the dangers of injecting the Covid vaccine into the human body and the agenda behind it, Brian called for a campfire meeting. In the meeting, while sipping on Jameson Irish Whiskey, Brian seemed to bear his soul. I don't remember all of the topics he addressed that night, but I brought up the topic of structure for the convoy. He replied to me, saying, "If you are thinking about structure, you are thinking wrong."

I was taken aback by this statement, as I knew structure was the only thing that would keep this movement from falling apart. I didn't follow up after this, and maybe I should have, because the convoy by now was hanging on by a thread. It was only a matter of time at this point before everything would fall apart, and I think Brian knew this because less than a week later, the convoy headed west to California to protest 10 tyrannical bills the California State Legislature was voting on.

Brian would not accompany us but showed up to speak on stage at the Defeat the Mandate Rally in Los Angeles, sharing the stage with Mike Landis, who found his motivational speaking voice by the time the convoy reached California. Many of us were extremely disappointed with Brian after Hagerstown, but the fact of the matter is, he did what God intended him to do during that time. The convoy would never be the same after Hagerstown. Still, looking back, there were some really spiritual and genuinely loving moments of people of all different races, creeds, religions, and political ideologies. Even though the movement lasted a short period, the memories would last a lifetime.

BRIGHT LIGHT
NEWS
Dr. Robert Malone, MD, MS
Inventor of mRNA & DNA vaccination

ORLD FREEDOM

Chapter 15

On to California

Just a couple of days before we packed up and headed west, a small group of Canadian women who had participated in the trucker convoy in Ottawa, Canada, a couple of months prior arrived in Hagerstown. Monique Mackay, Jodie Ledgerwood, and Shari St. Louis addressed the faithful crowd from the main stage at Hagerstown. Jodie and Monique were both beaten and pepper sprayed by the Canadian police while protesting with Canadian truckers in the capital earlier in the winter of 2022. The protests were peaceful, as families participated together and frightened the Canadian government with their scary bouncy castles the children played in. I did not witness the speech firsthand, but Joel was there and asked them if they were interested in granting an interview.

Later in the day, Joel brought the three women inside Tony's RV for the interview. We spent a good 15-

20 minutes talking and getting to know one another prior to Joel's interview. At one point, Monique told the story of being separated from her two daughters, who were living in Australia with their father. She was desperate to find and see them. It's so funny how God brings us all together, even if it's for a short period of time, because I mentioned Scott Russell, my Australian connection who I'd only met two weeks before. I let them know about his platform on Facebook, how big his following was, and that I would get in touch with him. So, during Joel's interview, I was successfully able to reach Scott, and he agreed to a group meeting with all of us that night. Monique's eyes lit up after hearing this.

Prior to our group meeting with Scott, Shari explained further what group she was a part of. She partnered with a couple of other patriotic Canadians and formed the group Take Action Canada in response to the tyrannical Covid mandates. It was a platform that brought other organizations together in unison to show unity across the board to fight against these mandates. Scott later coined the phrase "We Move As One" after he agreed to set up Take Action Australia, and this was soon used universally.

As Shari continued by explaining what exactly Take Action Canada's goals were, the five Americans in the group all agreed that we wanted to be a part of something like this. So, after all of the discussion took place, Tony, Joel, Boyd, Rebecca, and I all agreed to take part and get started on a group like this for America. Tony, being the money guy, would finance whatever was needed until we could receive donations to help the organization along. Since I had set up an organizational structure for the convoy, Tony would want to use my skills to set up an organizational structure for Take Action America. Shari then set up a group meeting with the Canadian Team Project Manager and then we began working. We didn't do much while we were still in the convoy, however, until we reached California, except to participate in weekly Zoom calls with Canada to better understand how they operated.

A couple of days later, we gathered up all of our belongings and set out to leave Hagerstown. There were a good number of people who stayed behind since many felt what we had done while in Hagerstown wasn't finished. Truthfully, I felt the entire convoy was finished, because without that proposed structure in place, it was just a matter of time before the whole thing would implode altogether. Truth be told, I didn't think the convoy would even make it back to Hagerstown with all of the infighting, but it limped back after leaving the West Coast. So we set out and stayed in North Carolina for a night before I broke away to gather my belongings from my motel in St. Louis and rejoined the convoy in Texas as we headed west together towards California.

Tony, Joel, Boyd, and I traveled to California together, while Rebecca stayed behind in Maryland, at least for a short while. I was to pick her up at the airport in St. Louis while I was there and bring her with me to rejoin the convoy, but unforeseen reasons kept her on the East Coast until she rejoined us in Los Angeles. On April 10th, 2022, I departed the Defeat the Mandate Rally early on, picked her up from LAX, and returned to the rally with her.

Mike Landis spoke on stage that day, along with a plethora of speakers, such as author Naomi Wolf, long-time news correspondent Lara Logan, and Dr. Robert Malone, to bring awareness of the tyrannical vaccine mandates and what the so-called Covid vaccine was doing to people. The People's Convoy trucks lined the streets of downtown Los Angeles that day, and the truckers educated everyone who would listen about the dangers of these government medical mandates and what they were doing to hard-working American families.

Four of us met up with the Canadian women that night as we broke bread together at a local restaurant. Tony and his wife Melissa parked their RV at a local RV campsite and graciously paid for us to stay at a motel in San Dimas that night. It was there I opened my soul to Joel about my experience with losing everything because of the mandate. As I fought to keep my tears inside, I said to Joel, "Do you know how much I loved my job?"

I could see the raw emotion pouring from Joel's face. "No, no, no, no, no," he replied. He could feel what I was feeling in my heart. I could tell by the look on his face. Joel empathized with my struggle, and I knew he wanted to help me in any way he could.

We all became closer during this time, all from separate backgrounds, and these different personalities were special. Rebecca removed her guitar from the case and began playing soothing music and sang in a language I was totally unfamiliar with. Everything was so surreal, and I enjoyed most of these moments. Rebecca and I had a close relationship, but when we disagreed, we fought like cats and dogs. I think Joel put it best when he said we were like siblings, and we had that sibling rivalry between us. There were times when Rebecca and I just needed to be separated from each other. She was 17 years my junior and some of the things we did really rubbed each other the wrong way. Still, I am glad to have had the fortune of meeting her, as I did with everyone in the group, including Tony, who I later had a falling out with.

Our days with the convoy were winding down, and with that more time could be used to spend working on the new Take Action America project. While in California, we still only participated in Take Action Canada meetings, and we didn't really provide much information. How could we provide any information, though? We were a group of five people beginning a new organization and not one of us had any experience with activism, except for Joel, and even he needed assistance with this great task. We needed someone with a vast knowledge of these things. So, until we found a Program

Manager, we would continue to struggle while learning everything "on the fly" about activism.

Joel began planning for a rally held in Sacramento at the Capitol Building on April 19th. Titled "Convoy to Sacramento," this was a joint event of two separate convoys, and this would be the inaugural event for Take Action America, as the trucks lined the street on the north and west sides. The event occurred at noon on the west side, while a similar rally was held on the north side. Both rallies highlighted the 10 bills before the California State Legislature on topics such as abortion and the illegal vaccine mandates the California Legislature was attempting to impose on its citizens. Joel received help from his good friend Candace, one of the lead organizers of the People's Convoy from its inception, leaving from Adelanto back in February. Candace also played a pivotal role in organizing the crowds on top of bridges in support of the convoy.

That morning, Joel operated as the Master of Ceremonies in front of a sizeable crowd of several hundred that featured guest speakers Steve Kirsch, an entrepreneur and philanthropist in Silicon Valley, Joel's mentor Neil Mammen, Mike Landis, who by now rocked the house with his speeches, and Cindy Sheehan, Goldstar mother whose son was killed during the Iraq war. I met Cindy that day and briefly detailed my military history. I fell prey to Fox News when they reported on her plight in an undignified manner many years ago before I was abreast of the illegal war America waged against the people of Iraq after 9/11. Whatever side of the political aisle one stands on, no one can argue against the human condition. Ultimately, we, the people, wind up paying the ultimate price of the political overloads who do not serve our interests. Cindy and I shared a lovely embrace. I can't imagine the hell she went through losing a son to an atrocity committed by those in our government; I can only attempt to understand the depths of hell she reached in her search for answers.

Joel did a wonderful job in planning and executing the event. He was extremely nervous earlier in the morning because there were some slight issues with the sound equipment in the beginning. He worked through his anxieties, though, with the help of everyone wanting the event to be a success. When the time came to perform, Joel, though a bit nervous at first (*who wouldn't be?*) knocked his first major accomplishment with Take Action America out of the park! We all were proud of Joel and his professionalism that day. So we packed up and celebrated our first success, and Joel made some great new friends that day.

The next stop for the People's Convoy was San Francisco and Oakland. This would be the last leg of the journey for us before breaking off and committing our time to Take Action America. I cannot conclude the Sacramento leg of the journey without talking about something totally random happening, as was the case in much of my journey. Joel, Rebecca, and I stopped at a gas station not far from the California capital. While inside, I was approached by an older man who appeared to be in his latter 60s, wearing a "Retired Air Force" ball cap on his head. I was standing near the counter when he approached me, asking, "Is that your car parked outside with the military license plate?"

"Yes, it is," I stated.

"Thank you for your service," he said.

"And thank you for yours, sir. We veterans need to stick together in these times," I said.

He replied, "Yes indeed, we do. You know, my son works for the Department of Energy at Area 51."

Not really realizing why he would tell this to me of all people, I said, "Wow, Area 51, you say? I have not met anyone with ties to someone who works at Area 51. And the Department of Energy. The highest level of security clearance is the Q Clearance, which is given to members of the Department of Energy. Does your son have a Q Clearance?" I asked.

"Well, I don't really know, but he is not allowed to tell me what he does there," he replied.

I was really surprised that this short conversation took place, as it came out of nowhere with a total stranger and was completely random. That wasn't what surprised me, however. What really surprised me happened in the parking lot when Joel, Rebecca, and I were getting in my car prior to heading north. As this man came outside, he approached me and said out of nowhere, "I believe in 'Q.'" I remember this moment quite clearly, as I heard Joel scoff when he heard him.

I looked at Joel, smiled, and then addressed the man. "This is an epic fight, and it has ruined many lives, but in the end, I believe the election was a sting operation by Trump and the Q Team that will reveal itself in the end." To that end we said our goodbyes and departed the gas station.

I cannot stress enough how God is in control of everything and how He uses us in this game of life. Situations like the one I just described are little pieces of the overall puzzle coming together in this spiritual conflict, spilling out all over the third-dimensional realm. These little pieces that reveal themselves, I believe, are the small doses of "hopium" that are necessary to assist us in overcoming hardships during the most difficult times. God is always communicating with us, but the question lies within asking if we are listening. Are we dialed in?

We continued north with the convoy and arrived in Oakland. On April 22nd, we convoyed in the neighborhood of Buffy Wicks, a member of the California State Legislature and a target of the convoy for her part in the 10 tyrannical bills presented before the legislature. She sponsored AB1993, which would require all workers in the state to receive the COVID-19 vaccine (a snapshot of these bills is pictured at the end of the chapter). The convoy, still consisting of a sizable amount of trucks, RVs and cars, made three passes through the neighborhood to bring awareness to ordinary citizens about the dangerous path California was heading in with the passage of these bills. By the third pass, the citizens, who claim to be tolerant, showed their true colors, pelting eggs at the convoy.

There is great footage on YouTube of my car being pelted with eggs. I also recorded the egg throwing from the inside of my car as I hummed while filming leftist hate shown in a marvelous display. The eggs did their job and made permanent marks in the paint. A few of us continued on later to protest outside of Nancy Pelosi's house at the top of a hill in San Francisco. I really was having the time of my life, even though I was assaulted by "tolerant" people hours earlier.

After San Francisco and Oakland, the convoy headed up Interstate 5 towards Portland, Oregon, the next stop on the list for the People's Convoy. Joel, Rebecca, and I departed the convoy at Mt. Shasta, California, where I would stay at Joel's house before heading north to reconnect with Tony in Washington. My time with the People's Convoy was filled with a wide range of emotions to go along with the many highs and lows. I made lifelong friends from this experience, and though the convoy had some internal issues that should have been addressed, I think in the long run, the experience made us better people.

There are many other stories that can be told, and I hope the writers write about their experiences. Mine is only one, and there were so many more things I didn't write about that happened that changed the lives of those who participated. One of the things I learned most was that when united, the people are an unstoppable force. The question remains, though, will we unite and save this country, or will we stay divided and witness its demise? The choice for me is easy, but until we come together and set aside our egos, the status quo will continue.

NATURAL
IMMUNITY
EXISTS.
FOLLOW THE
ACTUAL
SCIENCE.

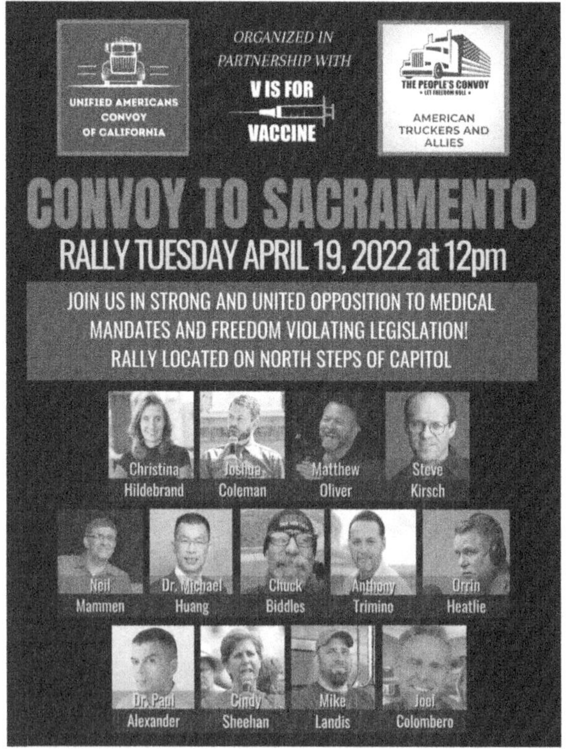
UNIFIED AMERICANS
CONVOY
OF CALIFORNIA
ORGANIZED IN
PARTNERSHIP WITH
V IS FOR
VACCINE
THE PEOPLE'S CONVOY
AMERICAN
TRUCKERS AND
ALLIES
CONVOY TO SACRAMENTO
RALLY TUESDAY APRIL 19, 2022 at 12pm
JOIN US IN STRONG AND UNITED OPPOSITION TO MEDICAL
MANDATES AND FREEDOM VIOLATING LEGISLATION!
RALLY LOCATED ON NORTH STEPS OF CAPITOL
Christina Hildebrand
Joshua Coleman
Matthew Oliver
Steve Kirsch
Neil Mammen
Dr. Michael Huang
Chuck Biddles
Anthony Trimino
Orrin Heatlie
Dr. Paul Alexander
Cindy Sheehan
Mike Landis
Joel Colombero

SILENCING
SILENCING

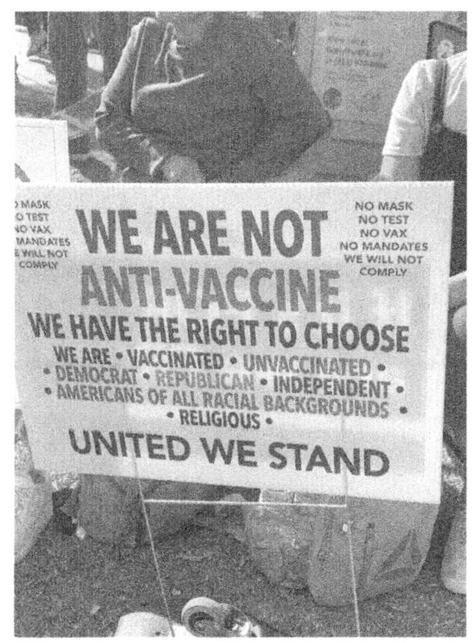
WE ARE NOT
ANTI-VACCINE
NO MASK
NO TEST
NO VAX
NO MANDATES
WE WILL NOT
COMPLY
WE HAVE THE RIGHT TO CHOOSE
WE ARE • VACCINATED • UNVACCINATED •
• DEMOCRAT • REPUBLICAN • INDEPENDENT •
• AMERICANS OF ALL RACIAL BACKGROUNDS •
• RELIGIOUS •
UNITED WE STAND

BREAKING NEWS:
#ThePeoplesConvoy is headed back to California this week to bring awareness to these evil bills.

The People's Convoy - Official

10 CA BILLS YOU MUST OPPOSE
VOTING HAPPENING IN THE NEXT 2 WEEKS

SB871	Adds CV19 inj. to list of immunizations for public/private school, regardless to FDA approval, no PBE, very rare ME (see 2098)
AB2098	Classifies anti-covid medical opinion as "unprofessional conduct" subject to discipline by the medical board
SB866	Lowers the age of vax consent to 12 without parental consent or knowledge
SB920	Authorizes the medical board to inspect a doctor's office and medical records without patient's consent
SB1464	Requires Law Enforcement to enforce public health guidelines or lose their funding
SB1479	Requires schools to create long term testing plans and report test results to CDPH
SB1390	Prohibits any person/entity from making statements government deems untrue or misleading by any means including on internet/ads
SB1184	Authorizes school health personnel to disclose child's medical info without parents consent to a third party
AB1797	Creates an immunization tracking system giving all government agencies access to vax records of all persons
AB1993	Requires proof of CV19 vax for all employees & independent contractors to work in CA

Chapter 16

From the West Coast to St. Louis

Over the next six weeks, we began putting the pieces together for Take Action America. The original five needed someone with experience in Organizational Management. We agreed on Joel's friend, Candace, because she was a trucker herself and someone with the experience of running a construction company. She was the perfect fit for the job. She was dual-hatted, both as a trustee with Tony and Joel, and Program Manager. My experience as an Inspector General would come in handy for purposes of transparency and accountability, so I declined being a trustee on account that I did not want any conflict of interest associated with my position.

Candace and I became close professionally, and we had some very candid conversations about how we felt the direction was going. We both felt that three was not a proper number of trustees, and a number of seven would most likely be a better number because it grew apparent her role as Program Manager would be questioned. This was after agreement by all that the Program Manager would be given proper leeway to run the organization without interference from others over the nuts and bolts of the organization.

So, after careful thought and dealing with a relationship with Tony that soured, I left Washington and drove east, not knowing where I would wind up until I received a text from a church pastor in St. Louis, whom I'd only had brief contact with before joining the convoy earlier in the year. I met up with friends Chris and Rene, stayed with them briefly, received an agreement with the leadership from Take Action Canada to reboot as Take Action USA, and began work on the next phase of development and recruiting.

By the middle of July, I was back living in motels all over St. Louis. I still had some money in my bank reserves, but I desperately needed to find a job. Chris helped me find a job at a Christian t-shirt factory called Elly & Grace, where I pressed a variety of Bible passages and patriotic designs on shirts sold all around North America and expanding into other parts of the world. The salary was a meager $12 an hour and was not nearly enough to offset my monthly motel bills, but it was enough to buy me some time while we built the organization. Lauri, my boss, was an exceptional lady with a very big heart. She worked very hard and helped all of the employees out. I was the only male employee, but the women all made me feel right at home, and they had some of the most dedicated work ethic I had seen to date.

While in Washington, I came up with an organizational structure plan that I thought might work. I kept in mind that we needed to be a grassroots organization, so I used the map of the United States and broke it down into nine regions. I used the very same map used by the CDC and the WHO and broke everything down from national, regional, and state. Those at the state level would be tasked with breaking things down county by county. This was a daunting task, as we were building a peaceful army to oppose the medical tyranny not only across the country but across the world. For this to work, tens of thousands of positions would need to be filled, and each level would give assistance when requested to help fill positions.

My emotions were on a roller coaster at this time. I no longer knew the city I grew up in. The friends I grew up with had their own lives and families. I felt like a stranger and was alone. God was the only thing keeping me together. By now, Min and I were no longer in contact. It happened while I was in Washington. She finally had a date for her divorce set, but a lot was going on in her head. She broke things off and went radio silent. Between the loss of her and the job I was currently working, things seemed to be heading in a downward spiral. I was okay when I was doing something so I could keep my mind off of things that brought me down, but when I was idle, depression took hold like a leech attached to one's body.

During the latter part of July, I believe on the 24th, as I lay in bed contemplating my life and where it was going, I prayed to God for someone special in my life. It had been way too long since I felt the touch of a woman, and I was very lonely on this journey. I all too often had a difficult time presenting a smile on my face, not letting anyone know what I was really feeling on the inside. It was a Thursday morning, and I had two more days of the work week to go, sixteen hours in total on my feet. Late that night, I received a message from Anna on Facebook. She would become an important part of my journey.

Earlier in the year, at the Defeat the Mandate Rally in Los Angeles, I conducted a livestream video over Facebook, and Anna reached out with a friend request. I accepted quite a few friend requests doing livestream videos over Facebook while I was a part of the People's Convoy, and every now and then, I would connect with Anna for short messages. We interacted normally the way folks would interact, commenting on certain posts, liking, etc. At one point in the summer, Anna showed interest in helping out in whatever way she could with Take Action Canada since she lived in Edmonton, located in the Province of Alberta. So I attempted unsuccessfully to put her in touch with someone. Though it never panned out, we began a close friendship when she messaged me that evening. We had a friendly back and forth for a couple of hours that evening, and we really seemed to connect.

In the beginning, we kept our communications to instant messenger. I felt that each of us was feeling the other out, but I sensed she wanted to communicate more than just through text messages. I opened up to her like I hadn't opened up to a woman in a long time. I'm not sure Min even understood the depths of my despair because there was a communication barrier because of the different languages. It wasn't long before Anna and I would talk every day over text. Within a few days of that connection, we were talking every evening after I came home from work. I had to balance my time between the nightly conversations with Candace, as she was working her tail off trying to make connections to get TAUSA off the ground, so Anna and I would normally chat later in the evening when I was free.

It seemed that Anna and I both were lonely during this period, and she found herself moving from place to place the same as I did. I prayed to God, and He answered me, the same day, I requested a girlfriend. Getting in touch with her through God would come in handy because during the first week of August, Elly & Grace shut down production, and I lay in my bed virtually all day most days that week until the evening. My depression was so bad that week, and I truly didn't know if I could make it since I was idle with nothing to do and completely out of my element in St. Louis. I remember being hesitant to do a video with her because of the depths of despair I found myself in.

Finally, on the 3rd of August, I agreed to a video chat. We talked for a couple of hours. Our previous texting helped the conversation along. I was completely honest about the way I felt, and I thanked her for being there for me. I told her what happened more than a week before our video call when I prayed God would send someone into my life. We were like two peas in a pod and could finish each other's sentences. By the 7th of August, we were chatting by video on a nightly basis, and sometimes the chats were multiple times a night. Life wasn't easy, but I was beginning a friendship that would quickly turn into a relationship.

Meanwhile, TAUSA was having difficulty getting the website together. Candace was given a contact name back in June by a pastor she knew of a reliable person, who quite frankly wasn't reliable, and continued to drag his feet. Week after week, during the meetings with Take Action Canada, Candace and I had the embarrassment of briefing that we still didn't have a website ready to go. It was so frustrating because we were promised by this guy that we could use a website that was already completed. All we had to do was provide him with all the information we wanted listed on the website, and he promised to put it together for us.

Since he wasn't charging, it would not be his priority, but the minute he told us he was ready to go, we made sure everything was correct and ready to go, and

Candace sent him the information so the website could be completed. So, when he ghosted us for the final time, I contacted my cousin Robert, who had extensive experience with web design. I asked him if I could put him in touch with Candace, since she was much better at explaining to him exactly what she wanted for the website. By August 8th, Robert agreed to create a website for TAUSA without charge.

Having Robert agree to create the website was welcome news since I had a terrible day at work that day. The day was no different than any other, as I came to work ready to press the hundreds of t-shirts and sweat hoodies I pressed every day. My mind was really giving me trouble that day. I know my co-workers felt it because everyone left me alone. Normally, I would converse, especially with Kim and Toya, who worked on special projects behind me. I could feel the anguish I was putting out, and I realized anyone could read what I was going through that day because I just felt it in the air. I didn't treat anyone differently, but I just kept to myself. I desperately wanted a redo and wanted to start over in a much better mood.

I told Anna about it as well over video. As we continued our conversation, I decided I wanted to go to Canada to see her. We toyed around with dates, but I mentioned that I didn't want to commit to anything until I discussed going on vacation with Lauri. I figured it wouldn't be a problem as long as I gave enough time for her to prepare to continue production while I was away. Since there were no vacation days in the benefits package at Elly & Grace, it wouldn't be a problem going on leave, I just wanted to extend the courtesy of enough time to prepare.

The next day at work, I was a completely different person from the day before. As I was folding the shirts and hoodies, I whistled and hummed. Even though we stood on our feet for 8 hours, I wouldn't be surprised if my humming and whistling lasted most of the day. Anna helped put me in a very good mood the night before, so I decided I would go and see her in Canada. After talking about it with Lauri, I looked at the calendar and decided I would be away not less than 10 days. By August 12th, the decision was finalized, and I decided to leave on August 22nd to see her. Anna and I were ecstatic and couldn't wait to see each other.

So life went on with work, TAUSA, and Anna. Our video chats continued when I wasn't working and went on pretty long during the weekends. Anna told me I was different from any other guy in her life. It seemed I treated her much better than other guys in her past, and she had to pinch herself to make sure she wasn't dreaming because she just wasn't used to that. We were almost ten years apart in age, yet so much alike. We spent so much time on video, and we learned a lot about our personal lives. I told her about my marriage, my feelings for Min, and where I could see our relationship going. She asked me if I thought I would ever go back to Min. I told Anna that she didn't have anything to worry about and that since I found her, there would be no reason to try to reconstitute old relationships.

As the week went on, I realized Anna didn't have much in Canada. She moved from place to place, had minimal possessions that belonged to her, and needed me as much as I needed her. She had a daughter from a long term boyfriend, who she was no longer in a relationship with. She had some medical issues that were private to her, and I told her I wouldn't pry. I accepted her for who she was. She had an agreement with this boyfriend that her daughter would stay with him and his mother, who lived three hours away in Calgary.

The more we talked, the more I felt like bringing Anna back to America. She received money from the Canadian government, and I thought that since neither of us had many possessions, we could split the difference in living expenses until I found a better paying job. She wouldn't commit to that before I showed up, which was totally understandable, but agreed we would see what happened after I arrived in Canada.

There was something she wanted to tell me, and she wanted to wait until I arrived to see her before she told me. She kept saying that if she told me at this point, she thought I might think differently of her and I wouldn't show up. I told her that was nonsense, but if she felt she couldn't tell me at this point, I respected her decision not to. I'm sure my response made it more difficult for her since I apparently treated her better than any man in her life.

During this period, I ran into Ann Dorn at the local Texas Roadhouse at the opposite end of the area where my motel was located. By now, we were friends on Facebook, and I thought it might be a good idea to talk to her about a position at Take Action USA. I had seen her post regarding a fundraiser she was conducting on August 18th for the Captain David Dorn Foundation to raise money to buy needed gear for first responders. We met, hugged, and had a wonderful conversation before I went inside to eat a nice big ribeye dinner with a beer. I ordered a second meal to take with me, as Texas Roadhouse was donating 10% of all proceeds to the foundation.

By the time I was done eating, I came outside and continued with Ann. We talked about the Backstoppers Ball, our dance together and a few other things. I told her what I had done with the People's Convoy after leaving town the last time and mentioned TAUSA. I told her that it came to me that she would be an essential part of the organization if she chose to be a part of it. I asked her if I could give her name to Candace so she could reach out. Ann accepted, and we exchanged business cards before hugging and going our separate ways. I am really thankful to Josh McAfee for introducing the two of us, as Ann is a terrific person with a big heart. I called Candace immediately after I arrived back at the motel and told her Ann was interested in being a part of TAUSA. We both felt like things were coming together.

On August 19th, I received a message from one of

TAUSA's trustees about a matter. Vickie was a dual citizen of Canada and America. She grew up in Edmonton, of all places, the same as Anna. With everything happening at breakneck speed between Anna and me, I hadn't had the chance to let Vickie know until now. I told her of my plans to go see Anna in three days. What I hadn't considered was the changes in border crossing since Covid. Vickie told me she would check, but she thought I needed to provide a Covid vaccination card to cross the border. She said not to give any information on the ArriveCAN app on my phone. The ArriveCAN app provided the Canadian government with information on those coming into Canada. Vickie warned me against that because she stated that that was how the Canadian government tracked people digitally as they arrived in the country.

I remembered my time in the convoy when I received a blank vaccination card from Tony. I stuck the card in the glove compartment of my car, and it stayed there until I thought about going to get it. I told Vickie that was the route I was going to take. Yes, I was going to lie about my vaccination status, and yes, I believed God was standing next to me during this journey. I reasoned that the whole vaccination against Covid was a lie, to begin with, and we were fighting a multi-layered, multi-dimensional war against the 4th Reich and Satan around the world. So, I was not too concerned with claiming that God was with me and lying about my status of vaccination against Covid when the whole thing was an abomination against God and His children to begin with. I needed to put the card somewhere for safekeeping. So I opened the family Bible given to me by my aunt to a random page and closed it. I felt it very fitting that the page I opened was chapter one of the Book of Daniel.

Two days before my departure, Anna wanted to tell me something. She was very hesitant to tell me, so I pressed her. I couldn't think there was any reason that bad that would keep me from seeing my newfound love. Finally, after extensive stalling, she came out with it. "I have cancer," she said.

"Oh, my God!" I exclaimed.

"See, I knew it! I knew once I told you that you wouldn't want to come see me," she said.

"No, no, baby. That makes me want to come up and see you that much more. I don't think anything different of you. If nothing else, it makes me want to love you even more. I can't even imagine what you've been through, and I know you wanted to tell me the whole time," I said.

"To tell you the truth, I thought you knew already since my port is showing through my skin," she replied.

"Well, I wondered about that, but I didn't think to research it, and I knew when the time was right that you would tell me. I haven't known anyone in my immediate family or friends that experienced cancer since I was very young and didn't know what to expect," I said.

So Anna proceeded to tell me the story of how she

had been diagnosed with cancer two years previous. I didn't ask too many questions, as I didn't want to pry, but I listened. I later found out that her cancer was colon cancer, but the medical doctors gave her a hysterectomy, which angered her immensely, as she didn't see the need for that. She told me at first, she received radiation treatments, followed by chemotherapy. She said at one point, she just stopped because she knew the treatments were doing her more harm than good. I didn't know the extent of her cancer at this time. I was being a sponge, absorbing the information that she gave me. She seemed fine to me, other than the occasional trip to the bathroom, but many times we would video each other as she walked to the store for her groceries.

I only found out later how serious her sickness had become, and it seemed to be triggered when she stayed in Calgary to celebrate her daughter's tenth birthday. The plan was to pick Anna up from Calgary and drive her back to Edmonton so she wouldn't have to take the bus back home. I now understood what she meant when she told me she and her ex-boyfriend had a deal that their daughter would stay with him. Now more than ever, I wanted to bring Anna back with me.

The next day after church, I went to Bible study. I had started Bible study a few weeks prior with a group that was highly spiritual in the Lord and not judgmental of others. I've had that problem with Christians in the past who appear to be self-righteous towards others and judgmental. I find that to be a big problem among Christians, as that attitude drives many people away from God, which is completely ironic and goes against the teachings of Christ. So many, including myself, can be better Christians, but it's not just that. It's more than just being good Christians. Anyway, at the end of each session, the names of those requested are written on a whiteboard, and prayers are said for the faithful. This was when I communicated my plans to go to Canada to see my sweetheart, and I needed prayers to get beyond the border since I was unvaccinated.

So, with preparations complete and everything I owned minus the few articles I had kept at my aunt and uncle's, I packed everything I had with me from the hotel and placed my belongings in the trunk of my car. I had my mind prepared to visit Anna and bring her back with the few items she owned. We would be able to return to America with essentially everything we both owned in a Toyota Camry and live life one day at a time. Early morning on August 22nd, I set out on a spiritual journey that I can only say was directed and guided by God. I have no other explanation other than that I no longer believe in coincidences.

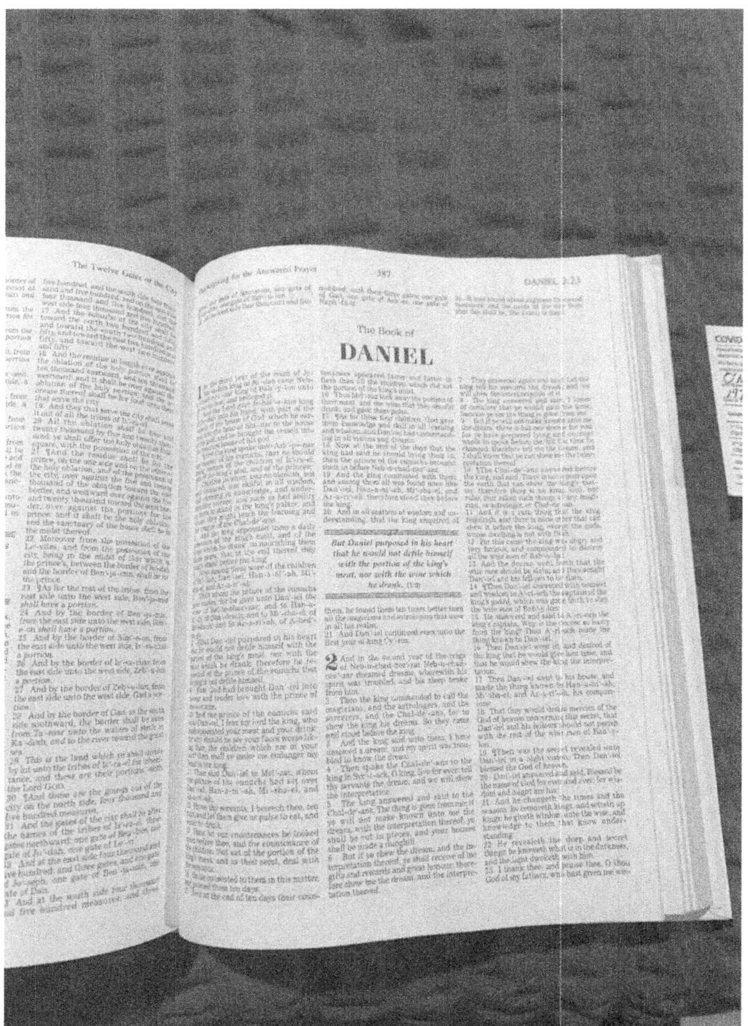
The Book of
DANIEL
But Daniel purposed in his heart that he would not defile himself with the portion of the king's meat, nor with the wine which he drank. (1:8)

Chapter 17

Dead Reckoning

Dead Reckoning - The calculation of the position of a ship or aircraft from the distance it has covered and the direction it has traveled without taking observations of the sun, stars, or moon.

- Merriam-Webster

Around midnight, I exited the Canadian border and traveled back into my country. Driving south towards Shelby was pitch black, and the rain was coming down so ferociously that I had difficulty seeing ahead. I slowed to about 35 MPH on the highway as I talked to Candace and explained the ordeal I went through. As we talked, she looked for motel vacancies but said there was nothing outside of Great Falls, MT, about 120 miles from the border. I exited I-15 at the Shelby exit and pulled into the Best Western to find out if there was any chance of sleeping in a bed. The front desk clerk confirmed Candace's earlier comment, but said it would be fine that I parked in their parking lot for the night. Apparently, during the warmer seasons, there is a lot of traffic back and forth from Canada and the US, making it impossible for weary travelers to find respite after a long drive.

While trying to rest in my car, I listened to the Bards FM podcast with Scott Kestersen. I began listening to Scott after the 2020 election. Most of the time, I agreed with his messages, as they were God-driven. I didn't agree with how he came to his conclusions all the time, but who agrees with everyone constantly? He talked about the challenges we faced in his podcasts and tied everything back to faith and the Father. I listened often and found his thoughtful opinions and engagement with guests inspiring. He talked about Gideon frequently and the victories God gave him with only three hundred men. That night, Wednesday, August 24th, I listened as he spoke of a conversation with another favorite of mine, Juan O. Savin.

Scott explained to his audience that Juan mentioned the Texas Reckoning Fest was being held that weekend in Mesquite, TX and said he should come. Scott had left his home in Oregon to travel the country and was meeting with Ted Nugent nearby anyway that weekend so that Scott would be invited to the Reckoning Fest as one of the speakers. This sounded interesting to me, and I decided to look into it once I reached my next rest stop later the next day.

I departed Shelby not long after the sun rose above the horizon and drove on I-15 towards Great Falls, Montana, where I stopped and ate breakfast at the local Perkins. I was visibly exhausted from my ordeal, with the obvious signs of anguish on my face. While I ate breakfast, Anna and I texted back and forth, contemplating the next move. I took a selfie and sent it to her, feeling totally defeated that I couldn't see the one person I wanted to be with. Never did my love or belief in God waiver, but I couldn't understand why both of us were called to endure the things we endured. After I finished my breakfast and the pot of coffee, I paid and departed Great Falls. I wasn't in any hurry at this point. My goal was to get to a motel somewhere to recharge my batteries and figure out my next play. It was obvious at this point that my love and I would not get the chance to be together as we envisioned.

At approximately 1:30 pm, I exited the highway in Livingston, MT. I was dog-tired and in dire need of a bed to sleep in. Thankfully I could check in before the normal time of 3:00 pm, so I dropped my backpack on the floor and immediately draped the covers over my body. I didn't want to sleep too long since I still needed to sleep overnight, so I set my alarm for 4:30 pm.

When I woke up from my nap, I researched the internet to see if the Reckoning Fest was something I wanted to pay for and participate in. Some speakers participating in the event were Mike Lindell of MyPillow, former Heavyweight Boxer David Nino Rodriguez, investigative journalist Lara Logan, Pastor Greg Locke, Juan O. Savin, and many more. The event would be hosted by Chris Eryx, AKA Baby Trump, who I had not heard of until this point. I called Candace to tell her that I planned to make this trip and knew I needed to be on the road early the next morning if I planned on making it there before the weekend. She didn't think it was necessary at first to pay the additional fee for Sunday brunch but later agreed it would be best to get closer to the influencers of the movement. She told me I had better get an interview with David Rodriguez, whom she was a huge fan of.

Later in the evening, I received a call from Anna, who was incredibly distraught. The mother of her ex-boyfriend kicked her out of the house like she had another time before. The two had a long, contentious relationship through the years, and the present period held no exception. Since the original plan of picking Anna up in Calgary failed, she was left with no choice but to stay in Calgary until Friday since she had no money until she received her government funded pension. I sent her money for a bus ticket back to Edmonton through Western Union (she wouldn't accept additional funding for an overnight motel stay), and she bought a ticket to return to Edmonton early the following day.

She returned to the house after she was kicked out, but the mother unfortunately did not relent, and her ex-boyfriend did not intervene between the two. Imagine having Stage 4 Cancer and being denied shelter by the grandmother of your child. Anna slept out in the elements that night, awaiting the bus to arrive. She was not able to fall asleep in the cold, as the evenings in late August that far north get pretty chilly. It is my belief that this night resulted in the point of no return regarding Anna's health because she was never the same.

The next morning at 6:00 am Mountain Time, I pulled out of the gas station down the street from the motel and began my trek to Texas from Montana. There were quite a few Bards podcasts I hadn't listened to, so I pressed play and listened to them continuously for quite a few hours. A few hours into my drive, while heading east along I-90, I passed a hitchhiker on the side of the road just outside of Gillette, Wyoming. Ever since I was a child, I never picked up anyone along the side of the road. It just wasn't safe, and in this day and age, it's worse. Immediately after passing the man, I heard a voice inside tell me to turn around and pick him up. I kept driving. The voice again said, "Turn around and pick him up." Having to go against every principle I ever had about picking up strangers on the highway, I thought that if there was an exit over the next two miles, I would turn around. Two miles came and went, so I kept on. Then, as I looked less than a mile later, there was a turnaround point in the middle of the road. God had been telling me all along to pick this man up. I was not going to argue with God, so I turned around, headed back to the first exit past him and stopped at a gas station, where I picked up two coffees and snacks.

I pulled up behind him on the shoulder and told him I would take him to where he needed to go. His destination was Denver, approximately five hours away and not really out of the way for me. It turns out there was a heavy downpour approaching where he waited along the highway. He was prepared for it, with a plastic poncho readily available to put over his body when needed, but he would not need it on this day. He was visiting family friends and decided to give hitchhiking a chance, otherwise, he would ride the bus back to Denver the next day. He told me the bus ticket would cost $71. I want to think getting him home early helped out somehow. We drove for five hours and talked most of the way. After I dropped him off, I continued on with my journey south towards Texas.

Knowing I'm a fan of 17, I decided to drive 17 hours that day until I stopped to rest. So at midnight, I wearily pulled into a Best Western in a place none other than Quanah, Texas. Here I was, trying to show off, driving from the Mountain Time Zone of Montana and arriving in the Central Time Zone of Texas, and the city I arrived in began with a 'Q.' It was even funnier to learn that the password to the wifi was 'Qtip.' This trip was beginning to look more and more divine as time went on. I even remained calm when checking in; experiencing two trainees on the midnight shift who made the owner lose his patience. The experience was pleasant, however, and the staff, while inexperienced, were a bit older and did everything possible to make my stay comfortable. In the end, I was only three and a half hours west of Mesquite, and I didn't need to leave early, so I opted for a late check out on Friday the 26th at noon.

Early the next morning, I opened my luggage case to put on a fresh change of clothes since I had worn the same outfit for two days. To my surprise, laying on top of everything in the bag was my *Joshua 1:9 Strong* shirt I had been given from my job at Elly & Grace. How prophetic this was that all the rifling the Canadians had done resulted in this particular item of clothing finding its way to the top of my luggage.

The passage of Joshua 1:9 states *Have I not commanded thee? Be strong and of a good courage; be not afraid, neither be dismayed; for the Lord thy God is with thee whithersoever thou goest.*

This was definitely a sign from God. One that I looked back on as being the reason I was so calm during my interrogation. Everything seemed to fall into place as I was completely *dialed in.* At this point, I felt I was a vessel used by God on this journey and I shared this experience with the women at TAUSA with a picture I took.

A few minutes after noon on August 26th, I departed the hotel en route to Mesquite, stopping at a fast food drive-thru along the way. During the drive, I called the number listed on the Texas Reckoning website to reserve a seat at the brunch held on Sunday. The person on the other end answered with, "This is Chris. How may I serve you today?" Chris Eryx, also known as "Baby Trump" was on the other end of the line. I had not heard of him before, but he was the host of the event that weekend. I thought it was very profound that he answered his phone so humbly. What a refreshing way to meet someone of influence other than to hear those first words. I knew reserving a seat at Sunday brunch was right, and called Candace afterwards to let her know about the experience.

I called Anna, too. I know she was happy to be a part of what I was doing, even though it was from afar. I talked with her for a little bit the night prior after I checked into the Best Western. She had been keeping in touch with me on the drive to Texas and let me know when she arrived back home in Edmonton. She was a little shaken by her experience in Calgary, but she was a tough cookie. Though she caught a cold from sleeping out in the elements the night before, the important thing was she made it home safe and sound.

I arrived in Mesquite late in the afternoon, around 4:00 pm. Mesquite just so happened to be District 107, and the Hampton Inn & Suites, where the convention was held, was on 1700 Rodeo Drive. In Gematria, zeroes don't count, so there was that number 17 again. There were three hotels in close proximity with one another, and the Hampton was full when I tried to reserve my room two nights prior. So, I reserved a room right down the street at the Holiday Inn Express. I checked in with the front desk, with none other than room three hundred assigned to me. I couldn't help but laugh, as it is so apparent that God has a wonderful sense of humor. So I brought my belongings to the room, relaxed, and talked to Anna for a while. She admitted being jealous of what was happening and wanted to be with me. I told her I wish she was with me too.

At approximately 6:00 pm, I ventured out of the hotel to do a reconnaissance of the Hampton to seek out where exactly the convention was going to be held. I was hungry too, and the hotel didn't have a restaurant, so I was hoping to be able to eat at Hampton Inn. It didn't take that long, and there wasn't a restaurant there either, so I headed to the exit through the lobby. I stopped in my tracks when I saw former heavyweight boxer David Nino Rodriguez. He was talking to a few fans in the middle of the lobby, while I stood near the front desk, watching in amazement. Nino was a towering figure, standing head and shoulders above the five people who stood near him. Standing at about 6 feet 5 inches, I couldn't help but marvel at the sight of this man. This was who Candace wanted me to try to lock an interview with, and I would have tried had he not had to leave early before the Sunday brunch because of family matters.

I left the hotel and headed back down the street to the Marriott, next door to where I stayed. I walked inside and searched before finally asking the desk clerk if the Marriott had a restaurant. After hearing they didn't, I walked outside. Standing outside wearing a black t-shirt with the words AND WE KNOW inscribed from Romans 8:28, with the logo of one of my favorites of the Truth Movement, LT, was Henry. I complimented him on his shirt since obviously Henry was a fellow seeker of truth and asked him if he knew of a place to eat nearby. He told me he was wondering the same thing since he was also hungry. So, two complete strangers hopped in Henry's truck and went to the International House of Pancakes to eat breakfast for dinner.

Henry and I sat in IHOP for at least three hours, drinking coffee, eating, and chewing the fat. We walked in about the same time David Rodriguez and about three or four other people arrived. While there, the two of us told our story to one another. I think Henry enjoyed hearing what I had to say, especially everything after the Canadian border. I told Henry I had no idea where this current journey was taking me, but I was prepared to let God lead. He asked me to say a prayer when the food arrived, so I did. It was choppy, but Henry said he appreciated it because he knew it came from the heart. Later on, while we sat there conversing, Nino looked over and acknowledged us, telling the both of us to have a good night. We both responded back in kind. We continued the conversation back at the hotel in his truck for quite some time. It was a memorable evening, paving the way for Henry and I to hang out together the rest of the weekend.

The next morning, Henry and I met inside the convention hall and sat near the front to watch the speakers. My friend Pioy, a US Army veteran who had a considerable following on the telegram channel *We the People News*, showed up as well. I opened my Facebook and proceeded to livestream so Anna and Candace could watch. Pastor Greg Locke was a featured guest who rocked the house and talked about the necessity for riders in the spirit of Paul Revere, warning others of the evil happening all around. This one hit Candace in the sweet spot, as she told me she felt that message was for her. It was beautiful to hear that, and a testament to the fact that if you listen closely, God sends His messages to you. After all, TAUSA was exactly that: a Paul Revere searching for more Paul Revere's to spread the message.

After listening to a few speakers, Henry and I bought Juan O. Savin's book *Kid By the Side of the Road* and waited in line to speak with him. The line was long, as Juan is very popular with many inside the movement, but well worth the wait. Earlier in the morning, I caught up with Juan in the lobby and showed him the ruby ring I was given by the General in Afghanistan. We shared stories about our ruby rings, and to my surprise, he could tell me where my ruby came from just by looking at it. In the convention hall, he spent a good 10-15 minutes with me as he sat at his table, signing different pages of my book and listening to me tell my story of how I ended up there.

The minute I mentioned Shelby, Montana, after my ordeal at the Canadian border, he told me about being pulled over in Shelby for going well above 100 MPH. He told me if I wanted to work again with the government, there would be plenty of jobs in the future. I shook my head to let him know that Take Action was where I felt I needed to be. Prior to leaving the chair, I pulled out a TAUSA business card and gave it to him. Using the same silver marker he used on the different pages of my book, he turned the card over, scribbled something on it, and placed it in his left breast pocket.

Talking to Juan was very memorable, and those who believe Juan is a grifter of the movement don't know the man. What I witnessed that weekend was something rare for celebrities. When he wasn't up on stage, Juan sat behind the table, talking to people and signing their books. He did that the entire day Saturday, all the way into the night until about 3:00 am. He continued the next morning during brunch, sitting one-on-one with fans until sometime in the afternoon. On Saturday, before Henry and I talked with him, we witnessed Juan spend about 30 minutes or so crouching next to a wheel-chair-bound Air Force Veteran, talking to him in private.

Later on that afternoon, I ran into Constitutional Law Attorney Tom Renz outside the conference hall. I waited patiently as two women talked to Tom about something near and dear to them. He saw me waiting in the distance, and I could tell he wanted to end the long conversation, but he was a very nice man who allowed them to finish. I approached him and introduced myself. I told him up front I didn't want to take up too much of his time since he was a very busy man, but I mentioned my friend Dwayne, who had completed the religious exemption with the approval of Dr. Nepute and himself. He remembered the interview he did where Dwayne talked to him about religious exemptions. I told Tom that as soon as this war was over, I would need some type of legal representation, but that I knew he was very busy working on many things at this time. I gave him my business card and thanked him for taking the time to talk to me.

The next morning, there was a sizable amount of us left for brunch. I saw a woman who was wearing a shirt that I made for Elly & Grace that said *One Nation Under God*. The way it was produced was with a line separating God and One Nation. Of all the places to see a t-shirt from where I worked, it had to be the Texas Reckoning Fest. I walked over to her and struck up a conversation with her about the shirt. She confirmed Elly & Grace was where she purchased it and allowed me to take a picture to send it back to Lauri in Missouri.

The tables were round and seated eight. Henry and I sat at the table with a few others he met that weekend. Gunnar and Lila Nelson joined us as well, Gunnar sitting directly across from me. Gunnar was the son of Ricky Nelson and grandson of Ozzie and Harriet. He and his brother Matthew sang together and had been touring the country since the 80s. We discussed Q and devolution together, to which I said I believed Q was real and devolution was in play. It was a nice exchange, and as everyone from the table got up and went to the breakfast bar, I approached Gunnar and Lila. I looked at him, gave my business card, and said, "I don't know whether or not this is the right time to do this, but my organization is looking for a spokesperson, and I would love it if you would be interested in talking to my Program Manager about the possibility."

Lila's face immediately brightened up, showing approval. Gunnar followed with, "I'll call you."

Shortly after noon on Monday, still riding high from my experience, I headed east to Montgomery, Texas, to visit Vickie and her husband. She didn't show up to the venue because Scott Kestersen canceled his appearance at the last minute. I told them everything I had experienced and said I didn't know where God would lead me next. My plan was to stay overnight before heading out. Candace was able to secure a meeting with Ann the next day, but I had planned to be on the road.

Unfortunately for me, the next day, I was sick. Vickie said it was because they fed me good, healthy food that shocked my system. It hit me like a ton of bricks, so there was no way I would be in any condition to leave the following day. When it came time to interview Ann, I could only listen, as I felt miserable. I could be heard off camera saying, "Hello." The trustees interviewed her, and all parties agreed to bring her into the fold. As sick as I felt, I was happy that Ann was added, and laughed when Vickie joked that she had poisoned me.

Not long after finishing up with Ann, Anna texted me letting me know she called a cab to bring her to the hospital. She was having severe stomach pains that forced her to go to the hospital. I told Vickie what happened, and she talked to Anna when I called her. Vickie informed Anna about her rights and showed her where to find paperwork to show the doctors to allow admission without getting the Covid vaccine. While at the hospital, the doctors told Anna she needed a blood transfusion. She refused, however, because there was no way of telling the difference between pure, unvaccinated blood and blood tainted with the poison. She was treated and admitted for an overnight stay. I found it precarious that the both of us had felt the way we did at the same time. I'm not sure if there was anything to it, but it sure seemed strange that at that point in time, I felt as violently sick as I did.

That evening, I received a text from my buddy Rob in Pennsylvania. I hadn't heard much from him since I visited him just before the convoy, so I took this as a sign. We already had a Director of Operations for TAUSA, but he was extremely difficult to get in contact with. We needed someone in that position, and Rob would be the perfect choice, given his operational background. I talked with Candace to let her know my next stop on this mission and told Rob I was headed his way.

The following day, still feeling sluggish, I ate what I could for breakfast and began the 1,500-mile trek to visit my friend in Biglerville, Pennsylvania. I stopped at a gas station to pick up a water bottle. As I walked into the gas station lobby, I noticed a big bottle all by itself, just below eye level, on the shelf called *Eternal*. I had been introduced to alkaline water and its properties months ago by Rebecca, so I picked this one up. Only after a few sips, I began to feel better. I felt completely better within thirty minutes of consuming half of the bottle. I continued to be amazed at the works of God, continuously guiding my way on this trip. I would later pass through Trinity, Texas, where I stopped on the side of the road and took a picture of my odometer as it read 118811. I witnessed a palindrome right there in the town of Trinity. As the music band The Grateful Dead would say, "What a long, strange trip it's been." It sure was one for the memory banks.

This leg of my trek lasted two days, and I arrived at Rob's on Thursday evening, September 1st. Earlier on Thursday, while driving, I missed two phone calls from Brentwood, California. A couple of years earlier I downloaded an app to my phone that screened calls from unknown numbers that were not in my contact list. I opted to not pay for it when the year was up and deleted it, but it continued to work and still works to this day.

I'm not sure if that was Gunnar calling me, but I did not hear from that number again. When I tried calling it, there was no answer on the other end, only a message and no way for me to leave a message of my own. I should have told him to leave a message, but I didn't think to do so. Even though I missed what I thought was "the call," I figured everything would work out in the end. I was happy to see my friend after everything I witnessed over the previous eleven days and was happy to tell him about my adventures. God led me the entire way, and I was happy to submit entirely to Him for everything else from this point forward.

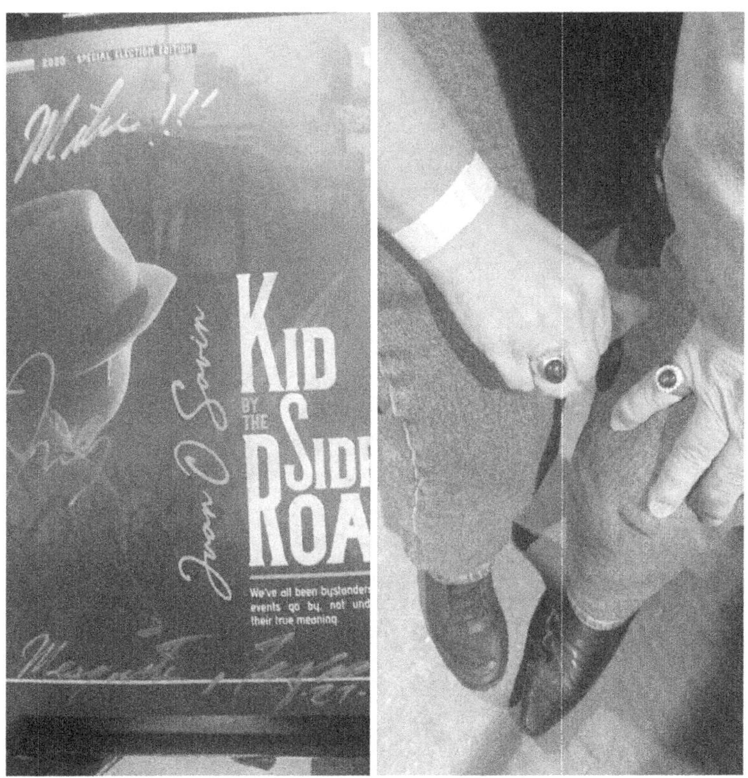
2020 SPECIAL ELECTION EDITION
KID
BY
THE
We've all been bystanders
events go by, not und
their true meaning

SAVIN
17

sherwood.tv
ood.tv

REVIVAL

Chapter 18

Biglerville to St. Louis and Back

I was happy to see Rob that Thursday evening after a long drive that covered approximately 24 hours over 1500 miles from Montgomery, Texas. We drank Yuengling from beer steins outside on the back deck of his mother's house while cooking a couple of T-bone steaks on the grill. I told him everything, from Hagerstown to the wild trip that led me to him. I stated that I only moved at God's word, and that word brought me to see him. I only realized later the real reason I was led all the way to Biglerville was not the original reason I thought it was.

Be that as it may, I explained to Rob why I had returned only after receiving his text a couple of nights prior. Knowing Rob's military and security background, I was looking to find an alternative to the current TAUSA National Operations Director, who was extremely difficult to contact over long periods of time. I talked about TAUSA in detail and asked him if he was interested in joining the organization. I told him that we couldn't afford to pay anyone without donations, but after a time, there were plans to explore the possibility of paid positions since this was full-time work.

I called Candace and told her that Rob was interested in joining TAUSA. Candace was faced with a difficult decision because she was in the trenches with our director, and they were close. She knew, however, as an organization that we could not wait too much longer and needed to forge ahead. We agreed to give Rob a chance to interview for the position and provided a caveat of waiting an additional forty-eight hours after the interview in case one of us was able to contact our current operations guy before awarding the position. The interview would be held the next evening after the trustees met over Zoom to complete the finishing touches to the Take Action USA website my cousin Bob worked tirelessly on to go live by the time I was in attendance for the Texas Reckoning Fest.

So, for about 90 minutes before we met with Rob, the trustees gathered and agreed on what changes needed to be completed. There wasn't much that needed to be changed, though. My cousin did a splendid job in the short time he had to put everything together. With all the setbacks we faced trying to put the site together prior to asking my cousin, the website took more than three months to accomplish as a group and was listed as takeactionusa.org on the web. One of the projects I held dear was Take Action's Core Values from the MISSION page. Our core values were expressed using the acronym LEADERSHIP, and we gave a short definition of each. They are listed here:

- **L**oyalty - We are loyal to God, country, and each other.
- **E**mpower - We empower others to grow and connect in their communities.
- **A**ction - We take action against tyranny through peaceful and lawful means.
- **D**uty - We have a moral obligation to educate through our initiatives.
- **E**mpathy - We show those who suffer that we understand and feel the pain they feel.
- **R**espect - We treat others the way we want to be treated and always check our egos.
- **S**elfless Service - We are here to serve others before ourselves: the opposite of selfishness.
- **H**ope - We provide hope in our country, hope in our communities, and hope in our fellow Americans.
- **I**ntegrity - We do what's right, legally and morally, with honor, even when no one is looking.
- **P**rofessionalism - We conduct ourselves in the highest, most professional manner and live these values for all to emulate.

The values are based on the Army acronym LDRSHIP, but we added the vowels and tailored it to the organization. We agreed to emphasize these values since so many groups within the movement splintered because of ego issues.

After our work with the site was complete, we conducted the interview with Rob. I sat next to him only as an observer, as I agreed it would not be fair to have a stake in this. Rob spent the next few minutes talking about his background in operations in the Army and as a contractor working on the high seas. After fielding questions from the trustees, the call ended. The interview was a smashing success, as I began receiving texts of approval on my phone immediately afterward. All of the ladies were highly impressed with Rob's qualifications and gave a thumbs up to his entering the organization as Director of Operations nationally.

The next evening, Rob and I sat on the back screened-in porch, drinking brew and war gaming about the expansion of TAUSA. We brainstormed what initiatives could be added to our list. I agreed the adding of initiatives was necessary but maintained the belief Candace and I both shared that until our organization grew, we needed to stick with simplicity before adding anything we could not yet handle. Rob stated we needed to come up with a solid, no-bones business plan. He mentioned knowing someone with deep pockets who trusted him and knew we could bring on board financially but would only agree to fund anything of strategic significance. We discussed the topic of me staying with him at his mom's and collaborating together on TAUSA while getting work for me at Chewy's for additional income. He brought it up with his mom, and she accepted.

So early Monday morning, I departed Biglerville for St. Louis to gather whatever belongings I needed, tie up loose ends, and return to Biglerville for the long haul. My return would come a week later. First, I needed to see my friend Henry from the Reckoning Fest in Orange, Texas, for a few days. I agreed to come back on my return trip from Rob's to visit my friend. I arrived Tuesday evening, September 6th, and met with Henry and his wife, Lana, at a fine restaurant that served boiled shrimp and corn. Later on in the evening, we visited his mother a few miles away in Louisiana. She was a spitfire at her age and it was a pleasure meeting and conversing with her. We didn't stay out late since the plan was to drive to his beach house on Lake Sam Rayburn that next morning.

We arrived at the beach house shortly after lunch, and Henry gave me the grand tour of the property, inside and out. The view was absolutely majestic. The back of the property went a few hundred feet before reaching the shoreline of the lake. Henry's beach was pretty sizable too. I felt like God was giving me a glimpse of paradise through Henry. I took pictures of the view from the backyard and was delighted to see a beautiful sunset that evening. Henry left me alone to enjoy the moment. For just a while it seemed I didn't have a care in the world. I called Anna over video to share my experience with her. I knew a video of my experience was only a small part, but if I could give her anything to cheer about, I would feel a little better.

I woke up the next morning, feeling magnificent. What Henry did for me, taking me to his beach house, was just what the doctor ordered. I spent the next hour or so sitting on the back porch, drinking coffee and watching the flocks of various birds gather around the beach before flying away together. With all of the uncertainty I'd faced since leaving Hawaii almost a year earlier, this visit gave me a little bit of peace of mind. I knew the struggle would continue, but what occurred to me over this entire trip was that God had my back. No matter how bad my experience was, for some reason, I did not know yet, I was meant to go through the hell I experienced; all the while, God held my hand. I was baptized by fire and made into a strong soldier in His army.

When it was time for me to get back on the road, Henry and I said our goodbyes. I followed the route out of Sam Rayburn Lake set on GPS and turned left on Texas Farm Road 1007. I had to laugh because there was that number 17 again. I continued driving north on the back roads for quite some time through Texas and Arkansas when Rob contacted me. He told me that he and Candace had a really good conversation but didn't go into detail, and I didn't pry. I was just happy to hear about the collaboration between the two. We talked for a bit about our plans for when I returned sometime the following week, and then I continued my trek north towards St. Louis to stay the weekend with my aunt and uncle.

A few hours later Rob told me that he was given the nod to work on an overseas contract. He told me of the possibility on the first night, but honestly, I wasn't sure about the whole overseas situation. I was happy for Rob though, because he had had a tough last few years financially. God brought me to Biglerville for a reason, but as time went on, the realization became clear there needed to be a caretaker for Rob's German Shepherd, Whelen. So Rob arranged for me to stay with his mom while he was away. We didn't know how long Rob would be gone, but I realized I would be in a holding pattern for quite some time in Biglerville. By the time I would return, he would have already departed for his overseas assignment somewhere in Europe.

I arrived back in St. Louis in the evening of September 8th and stayed with my aunt and uncle for a long weekend. I needed to tie up a few loose ends, including a visit to Elly & Grace, to say my goodbyes to the ladies before heading back east to Biglerville. I had already talked with Lauri earlier in the week on the phone to let her know that due to my circumstances that, I would not be continuing to work, and Lauri noted that since the beginning, she knew that the job there for me would only be temporary. I visited briefly and gave the ladies the details of my escapades. They thought it was pretty cool that I ran into a customer of Elly & Grace in Texas at the Reckoning Fest.

I visited the church I attended while in town over the last 6 months on that Sunday. I continued to spread the good word of my journey, which would not have happened had I not left St. Louis to travel north in the first place. It felt like going through all that I had faced, both good and bad, was destined to get me right where I needed to be. I mentioned at Bible study that I would write a book about my experience. Little did I know that at that particular time, I was not destined to start it. I would need an entire year before sitting down to write, because the story was not quite finished. When it was over, I told Gene, leader of the study group, that I was heading to Pennsylvania, as I felt this was where God wanted me to be at this time. We shook hands, and I went on my way.

So the next morning, September 12th, I departed St. Louis on my way back to the east coast. I was going back to live with Karen, Rob's mom, and would help out with the dog while he was away. The initial term of service was 90 days, but Rob and I both knew that with contract work, it could be shorter or much longer. I would need to find a job upon my arrival because I needed to help out somehow without being an additional burden on Karen. Taking me in would be a leap of faith as well. Even though we met during Rob's tour in California as my commanding officer and the two additional times I stayed at her house within the past year, we would now live together. That showed how much trust she had in her son to agree with my staying under her roof for an unspecified period of time without her son present.

I stayed in a motel overnight in Eastern Indiana and departed around noon, driving east towards my destination. Karen worked part time during the week, with Tuesday being one of those days, so I wanted to make sure I arrived when she was at home. She reached out to me about 30 minutes before my arrival so she knew when to have dinner ready and told me that Whelen was awaiting my arrival. Upon my return, that big hunk of German Shepherd, weighing in at about 85 pounds, jumped up to greet me at the front door.

Unbeknownst to me, by the time I returned to Biglerville, my time with TAUSA would be short. There were a multitude of reasons behind this. First, after my return, I received a photographed text from my ex-wife from the state of Hawaii. I owed more than $7,000 in taxes from an apparent mistake made the previous year. This took a considerable bite out of my remaining savings, making it paramount that I look for work immediately. This resulted in dedicating all of my time to finding work, so I could properly assist Karen with money to help accommodate my stay. Finally, Anna's condition only worsened from this point forward. I talked with her almost every night until she decided to cut ties during the first week in October after she was given a short time to live by her doctor. I bowed out of TAUSA since I was now in financial survival mode. On October 16, 2022, Anna called me from the hospital, and we talked for more than 30 minutes. She was on morphine and didn't display any pain, and this was the last time we talked. We texted each other a few times over the next week, but when I called the week after that, her phone was disconnected.

Chapter 19

A Difficult Year

The year I lived in Pennsylvania was one of the most physically grueling years I can remember. I began working at an International Paper (IP) box plant about a mile down the road from Karen's place. It was an ideal place to work, as it saved me from having to make a long daily drive. However, the job was one of the most punishing jobs I'd worked in my adult life, and at 52, I wasn't sure how long I could endure. I started training there in October, and by December, I was working the night shift as a Strapper Operator. Right before box units were delivered to trucks, they passed through my station for top sheets and strapped by a machine that sometimes had a mind of its own.

The IP plant operated 24/7 and was divided into four shifts, with each shift working four twelve-hour shifts before having four days off consecutively. The idea of working twelve-hour shifts over a four-day period sounds great at first, but it's not easy work. Finding the right footwear to give comfort while wearing steel-toe shoes or boots can be elusive. I don't know how much money I spent on footwear and inserts, but the cost was more than $1500 over the year I worked at IP. During the time I was the Strapper Operator, I endured two broken ribs, a hurt wrist from all of the heavy lifting, two rolled ankles from not stepping off the step properly to clear the strap from the machine, tripped numerous times over the strap, and had bruising all over my body. I never reported the more serious stuff because I needed the work, so I worked through the broken ribs.

Working at IP gave me a profound respect for factory workers. That work, for me anyway, was, in many respects, more difficult than most of what I experienced in my army career. To this day, I find it difficult to fathom working there for years on end, but there were plenty of people there who had done just that. My heart goes out to them all because I know, for the most part, they do it out of necessity. One needs to be able to put food on the table, and the way I see things, IP pays enough for their employees to get by, and that's all.

That said, in my short time at the plant, I appreciated what management did for the workers. Many were disgruntled, and I would be too, but I couldn't help but feel good about what leadership did to try and keep morale up. I remember a couple of times dinner was brought in, and the factory floor was closed, so we could sit and break bread together. During Christmas dinner, the most tender Prime Rib I can remember was brought in, and I ate crab cakes for the first time. For whatever anyone thinks of the leadership, for me, I appreciated it. I guess one becomes more appreciative of things after losing everything, and though I struggled sometimes keeping up with the fast pace, there were many who stopped by to give an assist, including my shift leadership.

By February, I moved from the night shift to the day shift. I remember Dave, my supervisor, telling me he had never seen anyone moving from the night shift to daylight that quickly. Most of the workers at IP worked the night shift for years before a spot opened on the day shift. My job was an exception, though, since nobody wanted to work there. There were times that I loved the job, while other times, I felt like walking out. When the equipment was working, things went smoothly. But when something was wrong, which happened way more often than not, the shift seemed like serving in hell.

Most times, I came home from work limping. I averaged 30,000 steps a shift but I had more than that many times. Sometimes, I would burn more than 5,000 calories a day when we were extremely busy, and breaks were often challenging to come by. I was visibly struggling with walking, and my whole body ached when lying in bed. Karen and I sat together most nights to eat dinner, but there were times, especially when I was on my four-day break on nights, when I would not leave my room. She was gracious enough not to bother me, though it was apparent she would worry. Her son had gone through what I was going through, so she knew full well how to handle the issue since she had already experienced the same thing with Rob.

Truthfully, I was extremely thankful to Karen for taking me in while Rob was away. We basically were roommates, and I helped out financially wherever I could, giving a set amount to her at the beginning of the month and shopping at Sam's for our meals to augment her grocery shopping. We were far apart when it came to politics, so I avoided talking about those things as often as I could. I knew how much she hated Trump, like so many others on the liberal side of politics, so I never mentioned anything. I don't know what she knew of my support for the man, but I guess coming out with this book, it's now out in the open. Still, given what Trump supporters have had to endure because of the false narrative, I thought (and still think) Karen was a wonderful woman, but I didn't want to come near to the topic and drive a wedge in our relationship.

As 2022 became 2023, I continued to press on at work with International Paper. It didn't pay much, as I made well below half of what I used to make. Still, I was grateful to have a roof over my head and a bed to sleep in. By now, Rob had been overseas for almost four months, and things were going well. We weren't sure when his work would be complete, but contract work is funny like that. You could either be working for a couple of months or a few years, depending on what was needed. In January 2023, after finding out the federal vaccine mandate was lifted on the military but remained on the Department of Defense Civilians, I wrote a letter to Senator Eric Schmitt of Missouri via the Contact My Politician website. The letter was dated January 11, 2023, and stated the following:

Hon Schmitt:

I am a 21-year retired Army vet of two wars, advised an Afghan General and lived in Afghanistan for five years, followed by a five year stint as a Department of the Army Civilian Inspector General. I left Hawaii for St. Louis after being away 32 years in November 2021 when my gaining command in Korea changed my Final Offer Letter of Employment I received months earlier to state that I must show proof (sic.) of vaccination or have an exemption. This was two weeks prior to my departure.

Knowing that Hell awaited, I gave up all of my possessions and came home to St. Louis to stay with relatives. I had recently gone through a divorce from a 27 year marriage. Knowing I would be okay financially working for the USG, I signed over the house in Oklahoma (paid for) and gave my wife approximately 75 percent of my monthly pension. I have lost everything.

I spent the next year in limbo, trying to find my footing. Right now, I am homeless and am staying with an old army buddy in PA. I maintain a Home of Record with my aunt and uncle in St. Peter's. The repeal of the vax mandate does not include civilians. I am at the end of my rope, and I don't know what to do. I am hanging by a thread. I also want to report discrimination and ostracism by my former military supervisor at the USARPAC IG Office Assistance and Investigations Division. I need justice. Please help!

Sincerely,

Michael S. O'Neil

On February 2, 2023, I received a reply from Senator Schmitt:

Dear Mr. O'Neil,

Thank you for contacting my office concerning Vaccine Mandates. Your perspective significantly informs my decision-making and better helps me represent our state.

Our country was founded on rights protected by the Constitution. In our free society, we agree that our government should protect our rights, not violate them. These truths are why I have vehemently fought to protect Missourians from vaccine mandates.

Broadly speaking, COVID-19 vaccine mandates are unconstitutional and a breathtaking case of federal overreach. When the mandates were first announced, I quickly filed multiple lawsuits against the Biden administration to protect the rights of Missourians, including challenges to the vaccine mandates for healthcare workers, federal employees, servicemembers, and small business employees. These unprecedented actions would require vaccination or weekly testing. As promised, I never backed down to protect our fundamental rights.

And as long as the Biden administration continues these unlawful and illegal actions, I am going to be at the front of the line, pushing back every single time.

I will continue to fight for your freedoms as a member of the Senate. Thank you again for contacting my office. Your perspective helps me represent our state, and rest assured, I will keep your perspective in mind as I work for Missourians here in Washington.

Very Truly Yours,

Eric Schmitt

United States Senator

To my chagrin, Senator Schmitt did not offer me anything here. I considered his response to my cry for help as nothing more than pandering to someone he represents, and I let him know with my response. Working as an Inspector General, I was well aware that when a complaint was made against a member of the US Armed Forces to a Member of the House or Senate, the office would send a referral to the command to look into the issue. This was not the case here. Senator Schmitt did nothing but send a canned response back to me. On February 5th I responded to the Senator's letter via Contact My Politician website:

Hon. Schmitt: With all due respect, Sir, your response was canned. I brought forward allegations of discrimination and ostracism of a member of the US Army after I refused the administration of the COVID-19 vaccine because of an unlawful order by the man living in the White House. As a former Inspector

General, I can tell you I know allegations brought forth by a harmed party to a Member of Congress have been looked into in the past. I loved my job. I can tell you that the members of my former team would admit I was very good at my job. It was not an easy task to give up virtually everything I owned to walk away, but I would do it again. When I first came back to St. Louis, I toyed around with running against Cori Bush. I saw you when I was given an appointment to talk with Joe Lakin in Kirkwood, though I didn't know it was you at the time since I had been away from home so long. He and all of the local Republicans, save one, did everything they could to talk me out of running. I was at your opening on Gravois Bluffs. You were the former Attorney General of Missouri. What the hell did we send you to Washington for that I get a canned response from you over allegations of wrongdoing. I thought you were better than this.

As you can see, the response from Senator Schmitt made me very upset since nowhere in his response did he provide a plan of action, nor make clear his intention for any additional follow-up with me. Instead, I received a response to my second letter dated February 13th, which was a copy of the exact same letter that I had received before. I was completely beside myself. A Member of Congress, a senator, showed the true colors of his representation (or lack thereof) to his constituents. He was just another member of the swamp who didn't show any concern other than placating the very constituents who placed him in Washington D.C. to represent them. I followed up for the third and final time on the website on February 14th with a very short message:

Again, I have given you allegations of discrimination and ostracism by a member of the US military over the COVID-19 vaccine injections. Are you willing to look into these allegations, or are you not?

Sincerely,
Michael S. O'Neil
First Sergeant
US Army (Retired)

Again, for the third time, I received the very same letter Senator Schmitt sent the previous two times. This time, the letter was dated February 27, 2023. I would provide no further correspondence. This was a huge disappointment for me. For the Senator to not do anything involving my allegations was one thing, but to send me an identical letter three times showing how he stood up and fought for Missourians was not only an insult to me but an insult to everyone he represents. Since I realized I wouldn't receive any help using this route, I would have to try something else.

In late March, the 5th Circuit Court of Appeals deemed the federal vaccine mandate policy unconstitutional. So I contacted an attorney in the hopes of receiving representation, not only for the mandate but for a possible breach of contract by the US Government as well, for changing the wording on my Final Offer

Letter. There was a back and forth between us, and I forwarded all documentation to the attorney's office. In the end, no one in the office chose to represent me. I think one of the main reasons was because this would cost money, which I was not in much supply of these days. The office lights need to be paid for, and that cannot be done without the flow of money coming in. I could not pay at this point in time, and a case against the US Government is never easy. I now knew any compensation would only result from an overturned election. Many thought this an impossibility since so many were programmed by the media and corrupt politicians from both parties that the 2020 election was the most secured ever, even though the evidence against Biden's so-called win is incontrovertible. I still have hope, and I believe the truth will come out about the stolen election, though I still think it is a sting operation playing out. That is the faith I have that the Q Operation is real and it is in play.

About the same time I was dealing with Senator Schmitt, I was contacted by an old friend from my time in the convoy. I had been talking to my friend Marlena from Texas for quite some time and semi-regularly after the convoy. She had been communicating with Liberty Lauren ever since the convoy ended. Lauren and I reunited during one of my weekends when she was free from work. I met her family that weekend, and we had a marvelous time. She was less than 90 minutes away in West Virginia (one hour and seventeen minutes by GPS), and I desperately needed to hang out with someone since I didn't have a life. I knew people in Pennsylvania I could visit, but dealing with my anxiety made it extremely difficult to gather up the courage to contact them and see them. I even drove up to State College during this period but could not whip up the fortitude to stop anywhere.

Lauren and her family helped make me feel right at home with them. There was an interesting dynamic to the relationship too. Lauren's parents, Doug and Lynne, had been divorced for many years, and both remarried. Doug was married to Bonlyn, who we referred to simply as "B." Michael Snider was Lynne's husband, originally from Canada but emigrated to the US more than two decades ago. The four have all been parent figures in Lauren's life, and they all get together for the holidays and during regular times for that matter. There's a real love among this family, and I learned quickly to enjoy it. It was as if God was sheltering me during my difficult times. I couldn't have the conversations with Karen that I had with the Hawley's and Snider's because I had been too deep down that rabbit hole, and I felt strange that I couldn't bear my soul, but that's the way it was.

West Virginia was my safe haven, which was fitting since the Sniders named their home *Lion's Haven*. It was nice to be able to visit, not only to get things off my mind with the world but because my work was physically brutal, and I quickly realized there was only a certain amount of time before I could no longer handle the physicality aspect of IP. So, I enjoyed my stays and had spiritual moments, including the last stay before I left the east coast for St. Louis. I would visit Lauren and her family no less than a half dozen times over the next seven months and I was thankful that God put them in my life.

In early June, I gathered enough strength mentally to visit friends in Pennsylvania near State College that my family knew when I lived there in Bellefonte almost 25 years earlier. I contacted my friend Kristy, who had been a very close friend of the family and daughter of our friends. We stayed in touch over the years through Facebook, and Kristy knew I was living in Pennsylvania. I came up to see Kristy and her parents. She and I met for dinner before we headed out to their house. We had a good, long conversation, and I told her of all of my experiences, to include how my marriage went off the rails. It was good to see them, and I had promised Kristy that I would go see my former landlords, Larry and Janet, but my anxiety again kicked in, and I traveled back to Biglerville without seeing them. I would finally have the courage to visit them the following month, with the help of Kristy, of course. We had a very good visit together.

By this time, I had reached the end of my rope with IP. I didn't mind the work or the management, but the punishment on my body made it very difficult to continue. I had known by now that my time in Pennsylvania would be over by the end of September. That was the information I was getting in my prayers anyway.

There was no other way of knowing that I was leaving then, but I just knew after a year of living with Karen, my time there would end. I didn't know if I could make it to work through the second week of August, however. I had been ready to quit since late May, but I pressed on. By the time the end of June rolled around, I felt like I could finish up the last day of August, so I continued with the physical punishment. After all, I had endured months of the pounding, and I knew by now I could do two more months. So, I looked on the calendar and counted the amount of working days I had until August 30th.

The day finally came to end my employment with International Paper. There were quite a few people who came by and talked to me. I really appreciated the experience there, as it gave me experience with the difficulties of factory work. I have so much respect for the people who subject themselves to that kind of work for the little pay they receive. The salary amount there was better than many other local places, but the employees deserve so much more for what they do. I clocked out for the final time at 6:00 pm on August 30th and began my month-long recovery, for which I still have a small amount of foot pain in my heels.

I decided to write this story the day before Karen went on vacation with her son and granddaughter to Ireland for 10 days. I wrote perhaps the first chapter the day before she left and continued on with it about five days later, after the Lord used Kristy to send a message over messenger to give me a little nudge. I didn't mention anything to Karen about this, only because of the narrative many refuse to accept. My time with her over that year, though, was pleasant for the most part. She knew I watched entirely too much television, and that I cannot deny, but we watched many series together during that time. It was good to live with her over that period, and I will forever be grateful for it. In many ways, it was easier staying with her than it was with anybody else, perhaps because we were both alone and we were there for one another.

My time would come to an end, though, and I knew for a long time that staying past September would not happen because that was not the trajectory God had me on. I stayed there longer than I had stayed with anyone else, helped take care of Whelen since Rob was away, cut the grass that Whelen tore up in the backyard, and helped Karen out in any way I could. On September 25th, we hugged each other. I said goodbye to her and Whelen, then left her home for the last time so I could head home to finish writing. It was a bittersweet ending, pulling out of the driveway.

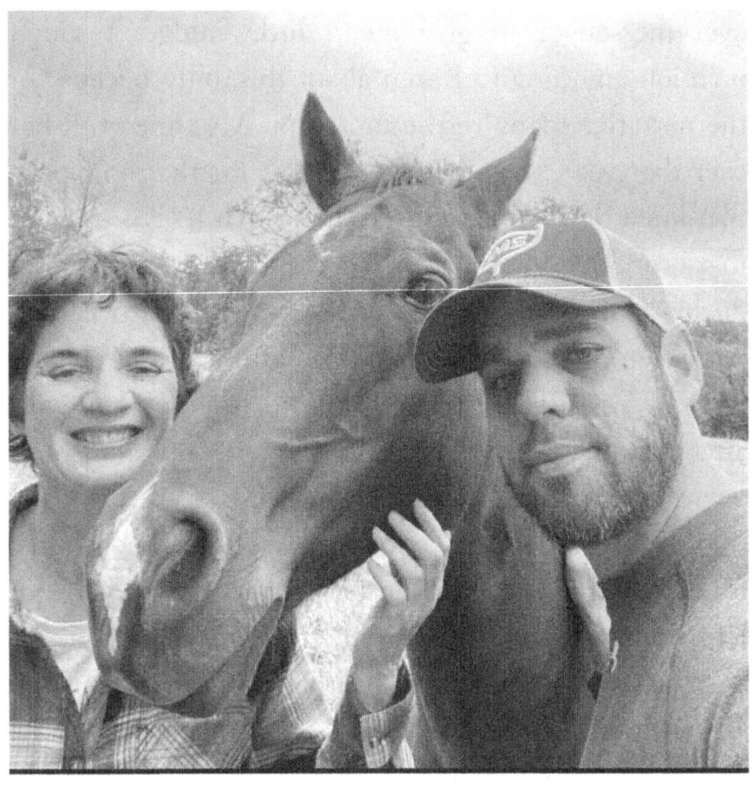

I am a 21 year retired Army Veteran of two wars, advised an Afghan General and lived in Afghanistan for five years, followed by a five year stint as a Department of the Army Civilian Inspector General. I left Hawaii for St. Louis after being away 32 years in November 2021 when my gaining command in Korea changed my Final Offer Letter of Employment I received months earlier to state that I must show prof of vaccination or have an exemption. This was two weeks prior to my departure.

Knowing that Hell awaited, I gave up all of my possessions and came home to St. Louis to stay with relatives. I had recently gone through a divorce from a 27 year marriage. Knowing I would be okay financially working for the USG, I signed over the house in Oklahoma (paid for) and gave my wife approximately 75 percent of my monthly pension. I have lost everything.

I spent the next year in limbo, trying to find my footing. Right now I am homeless and am staying with an old Army buddy in PA. I maintain Home of Record with my aunt and Uncle in St. Peter's. The repeal of the vax mandate does not include civilians. I am at the end of my rope and I don't know what to do. I am hanging on by a thread. I also want to report discrimination and ostracism by my former military supervisor at the USARPAC IG Office Assistance and Investigation Division. I need justice. Please help!

Sincerely,

Michael S. O'Neil

moneil5150

11 JAN 2023
First letter

EMPLOYMENT | EQUAL RIGHTS | ETHICS

JUMP TO FIRST MESSAGE

HOW IT WORKS (/HOME/HOW-IT-WORKS) | WHY CONTACT MY POLITICIAN? (/HOME/WHY-CONTACT-MY-POLITICIAN) | FAQ (/HOME/FAQ) | CONTACT US (/HOME/CONTACT-U

ABOUT US (/HOME/ABOUT-US)

Sitemap (/home/sitemap) | Terms and Conditions (/home/toc) | Privacy Policy (/home/privacy)

February 2, 2023

Dear Mr. Oneil,

Thank you for contacting my office concerning Vaccine Mandates. Your perspective significantly informs my decision-making and better helps me represent our state.

Our country was founded on rights protected by the Constitution. In our free society, we agree that our government should protect our rights, not violate them. These truths are why I have vehemently fought to protect Missourians from vaccine mandates.

Broadly speaking, COVID-19 vaccine mandates are unconstitutional and a breathtaking case of federal overreach. When the mandates were first announced, I quickly filed multiple lawsuits against the Biden administration to protect the rights of Missourians, including challenges to the vaccine mandates for healthcare workers, federal employees, servicemembers, and to small business employees. These unprecedented actions would require vaccination or weekly testing. As promised, I never backed down to protect our fundamental rights. And as long as the Biden administration continues these unlawful and illegal actions, I am going to be in the front of the line, pushing back every single time.

I will continue to fight for your freedoms as a member of the Senate. Thank you again for contacting my office. Your perspective helps me represent our state, and rest assured. I will keep your perspective in mind as I work for Missourians here in Washington.

Very Truly Yours,

Response from 11 Jan 23 msg

Eric Schmitt

United States Senator

Eric Schmitt

moneil5150

Eric Schmitt

United States Senator

moneil5150 02/05/2023

Hon. Schmitt: With all due respect, Sir, your response was canned. I brought forward allegations of discrimination and ostracism of a member of the US Army after my refusal of the administration of the Covid-19 vaccine because of an unlawful order by the man living in the White House. As a former Inspector General I can tell you I know allegations brought forth by a harmed party to a Member of Congress have been looked into in the past. I loved my job. I can tell you that the members of my former team would admit I was very good at my job. It was not an easy task to give up virtually everything I owned to walk away, but I would do it again. When I first came back to St. Louis, I had toyed around with running against Cori Bush. I saw you when I was given an appointment to talk with Joe Lakin in Kirkwood, though I didn't know it was you at the time since I had been away from home so long. He, and all of the local republicans, save one, did everything they could to talk me out of running. I was at your opening on Gravois Bluffs. You were the former Attorney General of Missouri. What the hell did we send you to Washington for that I get a canned response from you over allegations of wrong doing? I thought you were better than this.

Eric Schmitt 02/02/2023

My response to the 1st letter

moneil5150 01/11/2023

Eric Schmitt	Vaccine Mandate for DOD Civilians	
Eric Schmitt	Vaccine Mandate for DOD Civilians	

HOW IT WORKS (/HOME/HOW-IT-WORKS) WHY CONTACT MY POLITICIAN? (/HOME/WHY-CONTACT-MY-POLITICIAN) FAQ (/H

CONTACT US (/HOME/CONTACT-US) ABOUT US (/HOME/

Sitemap (/home/sitemap) Terms and Conditions (/home/toc) Privacy Policy (/home/privacy)

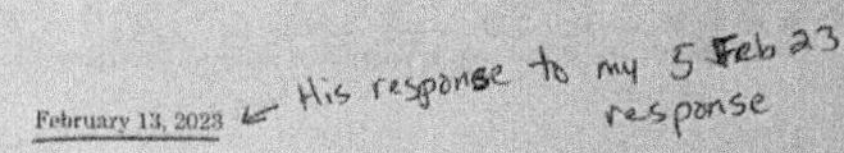

February 13, 2023

Dear Mr. Oneil,

Thank you for contacting my office concerning Vaccine Mandates. Your perspective significantly informs my decision-making and better helps me represent our state.

Our country was founded on rights protected by the Constitution. In our free society, we agree that our government should protect our rights, not violate them. These truths are why I have vehemently fought to protect Missourians from vaccine mandates.

Broadly speaking, COVID-19 vaccine mandates are unconstitutional and a breathtaking case of federal overreach. When the mandates were first announced, I quickly filed multiple lawsuits against the Biden administration to protect the rights of Missourians, including challenges to the vaccine mandates for healthcare workers, federal employees, servicemembers, and to small business employees. These unprecedented actions would require vaccination or weekly testing. As promised, I never backed down to protect our fundamental rights. And as long as the Biden administration continues these unlawful and illegal actions, I am going to be in the front of the line, pushing back every single time.

I will continue to fight for your freedoms as a member of the Senate. Thank you again for contacting my office. Your perspective helps me represent our state, and rest assured, I will keep your perspective in mind as I work for Missourians here in Washington.

Very Truly Yours,

Eric Schmitt

United States Senator

Eric Schmitt

moneil5150

2/5/202

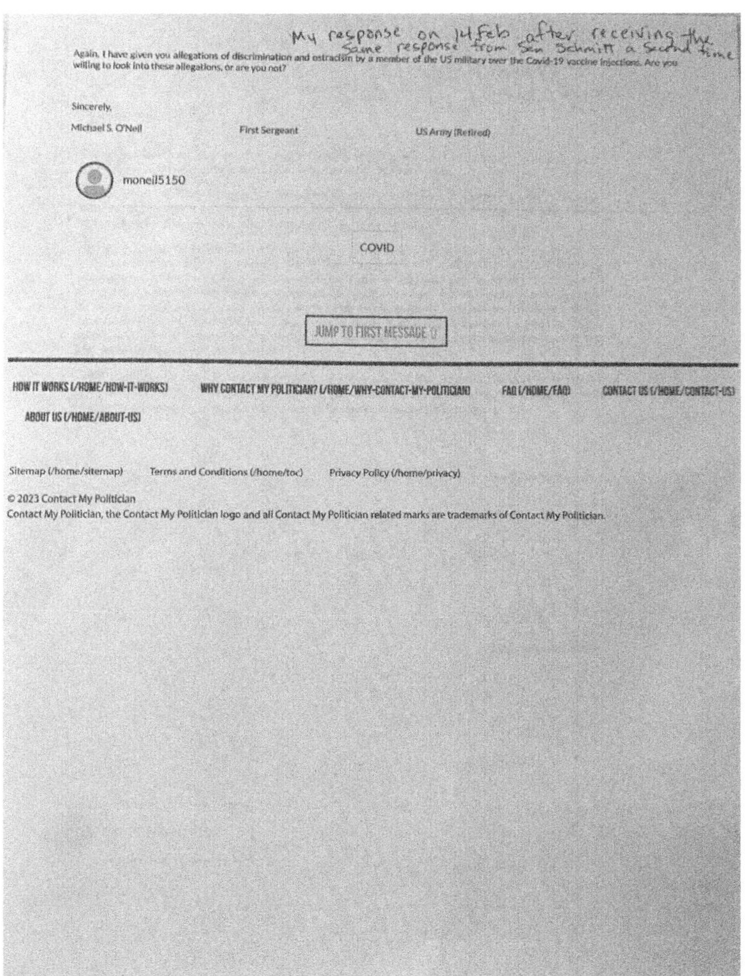

My response on 14 Feb after receiving the same response from Sen Schmitt a second time

Again, I have given you allegations of discrimination and ostracism by a member of the US military over the Covid-19 vaccine injections. Are you willing to look into these allegations, or are you not?

Sincerely,

Michael S. O'Neil First Sergeant US Army (Retired)

moneil5150

COVID

JUMP TO FIRST MESSAGE

HOW IT WORKS (/HOME/HOW-IT-WORKS) WHY CONTACT MY POLITICIAN? (/HOME/WHY-CONTACT-MY-POLITICIAN) FAQ (/HOME/FAQ) CONTACT US (/HOME/CONTACT-US) ABOUT US (/HOME/ABOUT-US)

Sitemap (/home/sitemap) Terms and Conditions (/home/toc) Privacy Policy (/home/privacy)

© 2023 Contact My Politician
Contact My Politician, the Contact My Politician logo and all Contact My Politician related marks are trademarks of Contact My Politician.

February 27, 2023 ← His third response. Same as the previous responses

Dear Mr. Oneil,

Thank you for contacting my office concerning Vaccine Mandates. Your perspective significantly informs my decision-making and better helps me represent our state.

Our country was founded on rights protected by the Constitution. In our free society, we agree that our government should protect our rights, not violate them. These truths are why I have vehemently fought to protect Missourians from vaccine mandates.

Broadly speaking, COVID-19 vaccine mandates are unconstitutional and a breathtaking case of federal overreach. When the mandates were first announced, I quickly filed multiple lawsuits against the Biden administration to protect the rights of Missourians, including challenges to the vaccine mandates for healthcare workers, federal employees, servicemembers, and to small business employees. These unprecedented actions would require vaccination or weekly testing. As promised, I never backed down to protect our fundamental rights. And as long as the Biden administration continues these unlawful and illegal actions, I am going to be in the front of the line, pushing back every single time.

I will continue to fight for your freedoms as a member of the Senate. Thank you again for contacting my office. Your perspective helps me represent our state, and rest assured, I will keep your perspective in mind as I work for Missourians here in Washington.

Very Truly Yours,

Eric Schmitt

United States Senator

Eric Schmitt

moneil5150 2/14/2023

Chapter 20

The End of the Beginning

I traveled down to *Lion's Haven* for the final time prior to making the trek home to St. Louis. I arrived in the early afternoon that Monday before Lauren returned home from her house-sitting job, about an hour or so before she returned. Michael Snider was semi-retired from a job similar to the factory job I worked at in terms of the 12 hour shifts. He worked Monday and Tuesday of every week. I sat with Lynne, conversing with her as I had done numerous times prior. Conversations between us came easily, and we talked about many different topics. She knew earlier that I came into the fold with a lot of baggage and gave me the nickname "Sarge" since there were many different Michaels and Mikes visiting *Lion's Haven*. It took a little while to get used to, simply because when I hear "Mike," I think it is I who is being addressed out of habit, but hearing the name "Sarge" really made me feel a part of the family.

Over the next three days, the extended family hung out together. Tuesday evening, after Michael arrived home from work, the Sniders, Hawleys, and I ate dinner together like we had many times over the past months. Most often, we grilled ribeye steaks, and a couple of times, we cooked burgers and brats. On this occasion, Lauren brought home some ribeyes. We prayed together in a circle while holding hands before our meals. After the prayer, Mike said to me, "The Lord told me that he wanted to give you a hug. He said you needed it." When we embraced, I closed my eyes and could visualize the bright energy beam that came down through Mike's body and passed its way into me. We both were engulfed with the energy of God, and it felt marvelous! This big, burly man towered over my stature, and we embraced each other for no less than two minutes, feeling the light and the heat of God's energy the whole time. I later told him that that was going in the book, and we shared a good hearty laugh together.

I departed West Virginia late that Thursday afternoon on my way to St. Louis. I had no interest in driving straight through for 12 hours, so I broke it up to drive six hours both days. As I had many times before, I noticed the number 17 pop up when I least expected it, and it popped up often along my trip. I never looked for it, but there were times I would glance over to see a highway marker that said 17 or 107. Sometimes, trucks passed bearing either number somewhere on the back. I know there is something special about the whole 'Q' thing. I can feel it in my bones.

On Friday in the early afternoon, I stopped at a restaurant in St. Louis to see one of my cousins. I hadn't seen Kathleen since my brother's funeral at the end of 1996. We grew up together and were only a year apart. I heard God tell me to visit her while I approached St. Louis. It turns out the visit I paid Kathleen came at a perfect time. She had been having a tough week and took some time to visit with her cousin. It was a terrific visit, and I look forward to more visits in the future. We gave each other a big hug, took a picture, and left the restaurant to drive the last of the drive to my aunt and uncle's, about 30 minutes away in St. Peters. Around 4:00 pm, I arrived at my aunt and uncle's. Neither party knew what to expect regarding how long I planned to stay. It turned out, though, that it was a part of God's plan. I would be around to help out after my uncle had hip surgery while writing this book.

These past four years have been nothing short of challenging for me. From the Covid lockdown to the shenanigans of the 2020 election, I still can't figure out how people didn't see the evidence of fraud staring them in the face. The following year, I severed ties with my former wife of 27 years before leaving Hawaii with virtually nothing but my car and a few bags. All this was followed by two years of homelessness, although I still count my blessings since I was always provided with a roof over my head. These last four years have been one hell of a challenge, but here I am, a survivor, and I scratched and clawed to get where I am today *only* with the help of God guiding me. This guide is a survival guide. I hope that my words can help those who have been through hell come back to life through God and His love for us all.

I have no idea how the next chapter will go, but I have faith that God will show me the way. I am grateful to Him for everything He has done for me during my struggles. These past four years have been filled with ups and downs, along with many twists and turns. I can honestly say that if it wasn't for Him guiding me through the different stages I have written about, I would not be here today. My only vices have been a little bit of marijuana and a lot of alcohol. I thank the Lord that even though I still drink, I don't consume near the amount I did when I was alone on an island. I have not been intimate with a woman in more than four years, but I have been communicating again this year with Min. I have no idea how or where that part of my story goes, but I am giving it all to God. He is my path.

As I wrap up this novel, I think of this as the ultimate survival guide. I am not an avid reader of the Bible, though I am keenly aware I should be. However, from what I have learned over these four years, that's okay. God will not chastise anyone for not reading His Word. From what I have been shown, if you open yourself up to Him, He will reach you in whatever capacity you will receive Him. You just have to realize that if you open yourself and your mind to Him, you can hear what He is telling you. Never give up! Whatever struggle you are going through, you will get through it. It may take six months, or it may take six years, but God will always find a way to provide the next meal, or the next shelter to allow you the next day. That's all we can ask for. I thank Him every day for my experience in this life. I know there are very bad days, but I remember someone telling me decades ago that when you think you have it bad, someone else you have no idea exists and has it worse. I am sure I do not have it worse than someone else, and I am thankful for that. I pray that those who do have it worse receive the help they ask for, and if I am ever put in a position to help someone in that situation, I will provide help with all my heart and soul.

I would like to thank everyone I have come in contact with in my life. We have learned from each other, even though some of the lessons have been ones that we are still not fond of today. I remember different times in my life when, for whatever reason, I treated someone a certain way that they shouldn't have deserved, especially growing up. I look back on some of those times with sorrow. I could have treated them better, which is most likely their memory of me. I guess the point is we grow, love, and respect the older and wiser we get. We can forgive others and hope they find it in a place to forgive us as well. I firmly believe we come across different people for a reason. Maybe this life is predetermined with lessons brought to us to see how we handle them. Many of which we pass with flying colors, while others we fail miserably at. In any way, I'm going to keep walking, keep striving to be better to others. I give complete credit and honor to the Man Above. He is the reason for everything in life. He IS life! He IS victory!

#SilentNoMore

bridge blue

(c)1999 Arnold Friberg

About the Author

Michael S. O'Neil grew up in the 1970s and 1980s all over the St. Louis area of Missouri. At the age of 18, he joined the US Army, where he served his country in uniform for 21 years, until his retirement in 2010. During those years he served in Operation Desert Storm and Operation Iraqi Freedom, and retired from the Army in the rank of First Sergeant. Afterwards, he served as a contracted advisor in multiple capacities to the Afghanistan Army from 2012-2017. From 2017-2021, Mr. O'Neil served as Inspector General for the Department of the Army in Texas, Korea, and Hawaii. Instead of taking the federally mandated COVID-19 vaccine, Michael opted out and resigned. He holds a Master of Science in Management from Thomas Edison State University in Trenton, New Jersey. This is his first book.

Made in the USA
Monee, IL
29 April 2025

16589743R00167